The Lost Book

of Paradise

THE
LOST BOOK
OF PARADISE

ADAM AND EVE

IN THE GARDEN OF EDEN

RESTORED BY

David Rosenberg

HYPERION · NEW YORK

ISBN 1-56282-759-6

Designed by Cynthia Krupat

10 9 8 7 6 5 4 3 2

TO RHONDA

Eve of Eves

ACKNOWLEDGMENTS

I am grateful for the Tamara Guilden Residency at Yaddo in Saratoga Springs; a residency at Mishkenot Sha'ananim in Jerusalem; a poet's residency at the Davis House of Fairchild Tropical Garden in Miami; and the continuing refuge of The Writers Room in New York. Personal words by the following individuals were crucial: Grace Schulman, David Shapiro, Jody Leopold, Madelyn Marcus, Phoebe Hoban, Walter Brown, Mimi Gross, Renata Miller, Antonio Burr, and Ari Buber in New York; Michal Govrin, Moshe Idel, Harold Schimmel, Philip Rieff, David Mamet, Shalva Segal, Allen Afterman (z" l), Amos Gitai, Ari Rath, Gabriel Moked, and David Avidan in Jerusalem; Bill Klein, Chuck Hubbuch, Don Evans, Amy Miller, Jack Fischer, Carol Lippincott, Nick Cockshutt, Suzanne Koptur, David Lee, Les Standiford, Mitch Kaplan, Mitch Chefitz, Jack Riemer, Jane Teichner, and Fred Witkoff in Miami; Trine Bumiller and Raj Parthasarathy in Saratoga Springs; and Rhonda Ramby in Houston. Lew Grimes, a singular agent; Bob Miller, Mary Ann Naples, and Lisa Kitei, special talents of Hyperion; and Shifra Asarch, inspirational mother, were key. Finally, I thank Grove Press for permission to excerpt from my translation of The Book of J, *and I thank Hyperion for permission to excerpt from my translation of the* Song of Solomon *in* A Poet's Bible: Rediscovering the Voices of the Original Text.

CONTENTS

A translator may "transform, enrapture, and transport," says the *Oxford English Dictionary*. To the extent it succeeds, translation blunts the memory of an original text. But the book I am about to present—*Sefer Gan Eden,* or Scroll of Paradise—has been lost and the surviving traces of it have been placed under a taboo of forgetfulness. If I am successful in imagining the Book of Paradise for a contemporary readership, the memory of its original text must intensify.

A few years ago, in *The Book of J,* I restored and translated a lost version of the Hebrew Bible, consisting of Genesis, Exodus, and Numbers. The biblical author, imagined by myself, by my co-author, Harold Bloom, and by other scholars to be a woman, has been designated by the initial J for more than a century, after her use of the name Jahweh (or Jehovah) for the creator. J's original text had been lost for almost as long as the Book of Paradise—perhaps since the ninth century B.C.E.—but substantial portions had been blended by ancient editors into the Hebrew Bible from which I translated.

The Bible's story of Adam and Eve is included in *The Book of J.* However, we know from Hebraic commentaries that an earlier Hebrew epic about life in the Garden of Eden existed, from which the biblical writer J drew. While little survives in the Bible itself, many further hints, references, and parallels of this Hebraic garden story are found in biblical commentaries as late as the Kabbalah of the Middle Ages. Early Hebraic commentary dating back to the ninth century B.C.E. in portions of the *Midrash Shir ha-Shirim* (or "Commentary on the Song of Solomon") names the two shameless and equal lovers in Solomon's biblical poem as Adam and Eve, suggesting that the Song of Solomon was modeled upon the Book of Paradise.

In order to envision the Book of Paradise, I had to go beyond the Book of J to imagine a lost Hebraic culture. Sadly, this period of great creativity is ignored today because biblical scholarship has become imaginatively impoverished.[1] However, some of the more talented writers in the Midrash, the early biblical commentary, had freely imagined the contents of many lost books, stitching them together with legend and moral fable. Their poetic instincts were still keen; creative inspiration had not yet been divorced from scholarship.

The Midrash is largely avoided by scholars today, many of them trapped in complex, repressive theories of what they call the Bible's "composite" text. Yes, it is composed of many different sources, they admit, but let's forget the original writers and put our imaginations to rest. Instead, biblical scholarship often resembles a knitting club made up mostly of men, hushing the conflicting voices and styles of the past. But history shows that hundreds of professional poets and historians, from the twelfth to the ninth century B.C.E., contributed to the new Hebraic culture, translating and transforming the work of older

---

[1]For instance, the six-volume 1992 *Anchor Bible Dictionary* is unable to deal with biblical authorship directly, even as each of its entries has the name of a contemporary scholar appended to it. And not only is this reference work unaware of its own irony, but its comments on "irony" in the Bible itself are empty of nuance and comical to any sensitive reader.

surrounding cultures, to furnish their own library. And this forgotten fecundity grounded the subsequent Midrash and Kabbalah, fueling their imaginative leaps at least until the *Zohar*, Moses de León's great kabbalistic epic written in medieval Europe.

Even in the founding days of ancient Hebraic culture, the archives of the associated tribes of Israel confirmed an older history and required professional writers to translate from cuneiform script into the new alphabet. In those times of ferment and discovery in agriculture, tree cultivation, animal husbandry, metallurgy, and many other sciences and arts, a writer absorbed and reflected this fertility. A culture, after all, is more than scribes writing in a ritualized literary language—misleadingly called a "world of biblical literature" by conventional Bible critics today. Not so long ago, theories of oral and folk composition demonstrated a similar bias against writers. Attributing composition to primitive inspiration, the world of Bible scholars tried its best to avoid facing the monster it feared: a self-possessed writer of independent mind—then, at the roots of Israel's culture, or now.

This much we know from the J writer of the Bible and the early commentary: Adam was given the task of naming the flora and fauna of the Garden, motivated by a quest to discover his mate. He assumed she already existed, since he saw that every other species had mates. All animals, even insects, were human size in the Garden, walked upright, and spoke. At least they appeared human size to Adam, who could not see or know anything of himself. Any creature might be Adam's reflection, or mate, until he examined it. As well, the divine consort, the *Shekhinah*, was an integral presence in the Garden: "The primary place of the Shekhinah was to be with the creatures below," relates the Midrash (Bereshet Rabbah) on Genesis. And in the beginnings of my research I discovered a crucial hint tradition has left: Adam and Eve had to build their own home or bower, an intimacy, even within Paradise.

The myths that animated the new Hebraic culture—about Adam and Eve, the first family, for instance—still underlie our own. Our reverence for texts owes much to this period, when respect for clay tablet and scroll prefigured the collection of many books into what we today call the Hebrew Bible. The writers in this formative period for Western culture deserve to be given back their human form. Adam and Eve too must be brought back to life in a living idiom if we're to envision Paradise.

In the eleventh century B.C.E., the author of the Book of Paradise was himself or herself translating an old creation tale. Transforming outgrown truths into new ones for a young culture, the Book of Paradise reflected an image of God as intimate family. Not yet comfortable with individualism, Hebraic culture composed mythic poems to interpret the bonds of intimacy. In the Bible's version of the story, two centuries later, the exploration of Eden ends quickly, but earlier, in the Book of Paradise, it appears to me that a relationship to nature was lovingly probed. The reader or listener learned of an interdependence with nature right at hand, closer than the sacrificial fertility rites of temple times, which turned faces heavenward, to commune with the sky god. In its encounter with cultivation of the land, early Hebraic culture as exemplified by *The Lost Book of Paradise* turned toward nature and to dreams bound up with nature's promise of change, which teaches growth. Change also obliges loss, and a later Jewish tradition grew from struggles to remember. That is why we find two versions of nature remembered in Genesis, one represented by a heavenly God but the other near at hand, represented by two of the most seductive trees in the Garden.

CHRONOLOGY

B.C.E.

c.2400 Early cuneiform (syllabic) tablets and scrolls in Sumerian libraries.

c.1650 Hittite libraries in the Middle East, including cuneiform texts and translations of Akkadian and other languages.

c.1450 Cuneiform texts translated into alphabets: Phoenician and prototype of Archaic Hebrew.

c.1280 Exodus of Hebrews from Egypt.

c.1200 Mycenaean Greek and Phoenician texts in "Sea People" libraries in Middle East.

c.1150–1000 First period of Hebraic books.

        c.1100 The Book of the Wars of Yahweh

        c.1075 The Book of Paradise

        c.1060 The Book of the History of Adam

c.1020 The Hebraic monarchy under Saul established.

c.1000 United Monarchy of David.

c.927 Death of Solomon. Reign of Rehoboam in Judah (Southern Kingdom) begins.

c.925 Editing of the Book of Paradise by Devorah Bat-David.

c.920 The Book of J (early Bible) completed.

c.915 Song of Solomon: J's revision of Solomon's composition.

c.850 First (E) revision of J. Beginning of taboo on early books, including the Book of Paradise.

c.722   Destruction of Israel (Northern Kingdom). Loss of early books. Rise of prophetic books (e.g., Isáiah). Assyrian ruin of Judean cities and archives continues. *Iliad* and *Odyssey* edited in Greece.

c.587   Destruction of Jerusalem and Judah begins. Loss of all early great books, including surviving copies of the Book of J and the Book of Paradise.

c.100   Editing of Hebrew Bible completed.

Devorah Bat-David

I, Devorah Bat-David, write in the third year of Rehoboam's reign. The new king is my younger cousin by fifteen years. When my stepfather Solomon, who sheltered my family in the royal house, died, I began to work with my father in the royal archives.

I was born in Elephantine in Egypt and came to Jerusalem with my family twenty years ago. My husband divorced me then, according to Egyptian law, and I brought the youngest child, Arieh, with me. I was secretary to my father, Ra Ben-Thoses, when he was appointed supervisor of historic documents. My mother is a Jewess of the ancient Jewish community of Elephantine, which sponsored the gift of my father's position to the new monarchy.

I became fluent in the languages of the Sea People, Mycenaean Greek and Phoenician, living for a year in Ashkelon and working in its old library. Recently I returned to the Ashkelon library, and there I found the Phoenician translation of the Scroll of Paradise, which was made in the period before the monarchy, more than one hundred years ago.

I have collated the Phoenician passages with the

ones surviving in an old Hebrew cuneiform text and here present a manuscript restored to a semblance of the original. My father calculated the place of original writing as Hebron, perhaps one hundred and fifty years ago, or at least fifty years before the Phoenician translation. Although I have found more ancient poems in Ashkelon that tell the story of the Garden of Paradise upon which the old Hebrew poet based his work, there are great differences.

The old Hebrew poet was intimate with the royal gardens in Egypt, for we find an attention to the domain of plants that is missing in the ancient works of other cultures. It was, in fact, Solomon's passion for gardens that inspired my restoration of the Book of Paradise. During his father David's reign and before, there was little concern with such matters. Yet in the ancient author's day, it was the custom to send the poets to exotic destinations and for their poems to be rich with foreign knowledge. The pursuits of settled kingdoms were exotic in themselves, for the Jews had been a wandering people and had not yet founded a kingdom of their own. Nevertheless, they had been planting in the land for many generations and had begun to cultivate trees of fruits and nuts.

Although we find in the non-Hebrew precursor scrolls the secret lives of Adam and Eve, there is little trace of the shelter they built in Paradise. Nor do the surviving texts concern the gods and the creator, Yahweh. But the evidence of commentary suggests there was a long tradition of archaic Hebrew paradise epics that focused on the characters of Adam and Eve in Paradise. In the Scroll of Paradise, the characters of the snakes are given larger dimension than we would expect from the commentary, parallel to their roles in earlier, non-Hebrew creation epics, where they were representatives of the gods.

There is a need on the God's side in the Scroll of Paradise for something better than heaven; he is unsatisfied with what is. But if there were passages describing this, they have been removed. We can only imagine that a problem with identity exists, since God's desire for an image to reflect himself proposes that he has already lost something. It is a standard theme in Canaanitish paradise tales that the gods seek to solve their problems in the world of men.

Yet we will discover that the problem here is with the divine consort, who becomes the Hebraic Shekhinah. She is revealed as the hidden force in the Garden, embodiment of Wisdom, and resides in the plants. The plants teach language to the creatures, but more importantly they are not selfish, for they instruct Adam in their concern to maintain all life in the Garden, showing him how to tend them so they might reproduce quickly and replenish the food that life needs.

Before our great contemporary[1] began her work, the poets in our age were often contemptuous of the

---

[1]Devorah here refers to J, the hypothetical woman who wrote major portions of the Hebrew Bible. Further references to "our contemporary" also refer to J and her work in the Bible.

past, thinking themselves progressive, and so they turned the story into fable, even a fairy tale or children's story, but lacking her wit. The complexity of heaven is reduced to child's play, with Adam and Eve represented as mere children in a playground. There is no tragedy and no growth, no loss and no memory, only the satire of innocence. This would be more moving if the tradition were remembered. When the Scroll of Paradise is read again, our contemporary's new history will seem yet richer.

The first man and woman, put into the Garden to tend it, must listen to the plants, for they hold the secrets of nourishment, growth, and the knowledge of origins. As we know from the old Mycenaean philosophers, civilization imitates nature, and this philosophy is strong in the book, where the knowledge acquired by Adam and Eve comes from tending the Garden. What convinces me that our old Hebrew author read archaic Greek is that the man and the woman desire knowledge of their past like he (or she, if the author was a woman) does, and this knowledge will require their leave-taking, in order to create an intimacy among themselves, without help from their parent Gods.

Now Adam and Eve will start over with the knowledge of loss; this is equivalent to a memory they have earned, a memory of loss. Here is an old Sumerian theme, given new meaning by the old Hebrew poet. If in heaven there had also been loss, the creator was missing a language to embody it. He was therefore re-creating the heavenly loss of memory in Adam and Eve. But this voluptuous Garden will not let them rest, starting with the work of tending and naming, and the presence of the missing heavenly partner will be revealed in the trees.

The writers who are now setting down the stories and histories of Israel are left with many shortened manuscripts, perhaps marred by priestly scribes in Saul's time or early in David's reign. These scrolls reduce the Shekhinah's role. The Scroll of the Wars of Yahweh, for instance, denies her role altogether, and although most writers today are critical of this book, all draw upon it for the new histories.

I expect that the God who will be depicted in our newest histories will be a surprise, for the writers all laugh at the warrior Yahweh. He may become more hidden, just as his Shekhinah was hidden in the Scroll of Paradise, for she was then a more subtle God. This will focus more attention on the drama of the people's lives, especially the families and the quality of love there. Our contemporary is fashioning an ancient family history in this manner.[2] The same inclination may have arisen in the Scroll of Paradise, where the role of the gods is supplanted by the creatures.

We have heard the tales of Adam and Eve in many languages, but our contemporary's new history is superior because it is written with the sophistication of our time. Although we learn little of Adam and

[2]Devorah refers to J's original version of Genesis.

Eve's own feelings, we are too modern now, after Solomon's reign, to imagine them as ourselves. Earlier generations truly believed they were children of that first couple, but we know it is tale-telling, for we have seen how the story is shaped in our image by the powers of great writers.

Far from being like ourselves, with secret fears and hopes, in our contemporary's new version Adam and Eve are presented as if they are children—in fact, *our* children. This is a believable history, given our power over the words bringing them to life, and thus our new tale supplies bare facts while sparing the subjective thoughts and feelings that fill the earliest Hebraic versions.

Yet there were many things taken for granted by the old Hebrew author of the Scroll of Paradise, things that the audience would have recognized in the telling of each chapter but that we have forgotten. Apparently there were earlier scrolls in which the snake and the tree were related, for instance. So I would be careful not to misjudge this scroll, for even if its lore is archaic there is much in its natural knowledge that makes for greater sublimity and subtler poetry than any of our day. Although it may seem fanciful to us, the minds of Adam, Eve, and the snakes may fascinate generations in the future.

Introduction

After extensive research into the origins of the Song of Solomon, I had gathered many unmistakable traces of the Book of Paradise, a book whose text has been lost for millennia but which is remembered by hints and references in early Hebraic commentary. I went to Jerusalem, to consult with archaeologists and historians about prebiblical Hebraic writers. I was searching for clues about the older poetic tradition that produced the Book of Paradise—a tradition I now understood had provided the sources for both the story of Adam and Eve in Genesis and the drama of the lovers in Song of Solomon.

With many related texts in hand, I began to imagine the words of the Book of Paradise while in residence at Yaddo—the former estate and gardens, now the preeminent American writers' colony—where I listened to tales of veteran gardeners, learning what it meant to "tend" a diverse woods. But at Fairchild Tropical Garden in Miami, where I served as poet-in-residence among botanists and tenders of the garden, I found the knowledge I would need to decipher the intent of the lost book.

My first speculations had taken hold in Jerusalem libraries, among bold imaginings about the lives of Adam and Eve in the Garden of Eden by the ancient interpreters. In their commentaries on the Song of Solomon, these early scholars assumed the lovers in Solomon's great poem were modeled on Adam and Eve, referring back to the Book of Paradise as *Sefer Gan Eden* or "Book of the Garden of Eden." Stimulated by the imagination of the ancient scholars, I thought about the influence this older book would have on the Solomonic poets who were writing major portions of the Hebrew Bible—the J writer of Genesis in particular.

The Book of Paradise would have been among many ancient scrolls during King Solomon's reign that received retranslating and editing by the court scholars, yet modern commentators shrink from speculation about this period and their Solomonic counterparts. Professor Michal Dayagi, the curator at the Israel Museum who studies the epoch, told me it was now a brand-new field. Hundreds of bullae, or replica seals from the period, have just been discovered in digs at the City of David and are as yet unexamined, while the scrolls and wrappings they served to bind have long ago disintegrated. These bullae most likely contain the signatures of court writers and scholars from the palace libraries, since the use of seals did not extend further than the binding of royal scrolls for another fifty years. (Later, seals were used in commerce and legal matters, so anyone might own one.)

I was allowed to inspect a few seal-impressions that may not become public for many years while documentation is completed, and there I found the signature of Devorah Bat-David, scholar in the Solomonic library. Because of our ignorance of Archaic Hebrew we cannot pronounce her name accurately, but its feminine nature is unmistakable. Moreover, it makes good sense that educated women at the royal court would translate and edit cultural texts; men, on the other hand, were more exclusively identified with the archaic religion and its ritual aspects.

Aided by a model reconstruction of King David's palaces and libraries, which were built before any plans existed for a temple, I began to imagine Devorah's life at the ancient court. In the street of coffeehouses (thick "teas" from the Orient were served) she would have joined palace writers and scholars numbering in the hundreds. Among topics for discussion would have been the huge influx of texts from India and other distant parts, a product of the booming trade at the height of Solomon's reign. No doubt some writers from the Indian subcontinent would have joined caravans arriving in Jerusalem, and it is just as likely that Hebraic writers would have journeyed outward to trade in scrolls and examine foreign libraries.

The contents of those early libraries, whether stone, clay, skins, or papers from plants, were plundered by ancient Assyrians and Babylonians, as were the catalogs and archival scholarship. But only through the eyes of a palace scholar could I imagine such an archaic text as the Book of Paradise in its poetic strength; the later sages, after all, had ritual preoccupations that would distort an impression of the scroll, coloring it with religious judgments. In their commentaries the sages seem obsessed with projecting ritual meanings into scenes such as Adam's naming of the creatures, while showing little interest in the physical and natural details of Eden. Yet nature was of paramount interest to the superior Jewish sensibility of the Song of Solomon's author, as I will later point out.

Also at the Solomonic court, living catalogs of tropical animals and plants—monkeys, parrots, exotic fruit palms—arrived with the trade in spices, piquing scholarly interest in earlier documents more devoted to the natural world. The culture of Paradise embraced nature and no texts were read in Eden, except that the Garden itself was a mirror in which writers studied allegories. My reconstruction of Devorah Bat-David's commentary on the Book of Paradise reflects a tradition of Hebraic paradise poetry that is discernibly Jewish in its emphasis on learning and tending—particularly in fathoming hidden knowledge—an emphasis that in later times was applied to commentaries on the root literary texts of Hebraic culture, although only those found religiously acceptable have survived. Devorah finds it reasonable that the Book of Paradise avoids the domain of the gods, just as does the Song of Solomon—but it is also possible that allusions to the creator and his familial gods were expunged by prophetic schools with contending agendas for heaven.

Witty and ironic biblical writers like the author of the Bible's J text or the court historian known as S (for his signal contribution to the Books of Samuel) would have been colleagues of Devorah Bat-David in Solomonic Jerusalem. And if I am right that J was also the author of the Song of Solomon, she would have had available to her Devorah's knowledge of the archaic period that was her specialty—one reflecting the qualities of personal independence and sexual equality that we find in Hebraic paradise poems like the Book of Paradise.

During the time I lived in Fairchild Tropical Garden—the only spot on earth that rivals for me the feel of biblical Eden— two huge rare palms, male and female, were pointed out to me, specimens that botanists have long thought to be the models of the edenic trees of knowledge and life. A species of Borassus, this couple's fruits bear a remarkable resemblance to human genitals, male and female. Further, the giant fruit has the taste and texture of prime meat, which prefigures the human palate. An apple tree, on the other hand, would be overshadowed by the lush fruits in a tropical garden; in European imaginations, the fruit of the tree of knowledge has historically been misconstrued as an apple (and in Semitic minds as a persimmon). In the same manner, an acquaintance with large tropical leaves, some the size of dresses, rights the misconception of the little fig leaves worn by Adam and Eve, as represented in Western art.

Beyond these small but typical learning experiences of tropical plants, studies with visiting scientists in the garden revealed ancient precedents for ecological knowledge that have only recently regained our attention. It was in talking with the actual tenders of this tropical Eden that I learned the wisdom of the dictum "art imitates nature," for the closer one looks, the fuller one finds nature sexualized. Art can only reflect the powers of seduction that nature unfolds, and in our deepest myths the mystery that nature teaches is imitated. For better or worse, a myth that works has a life of its own, mimicking natural mysteries. In the hands of a writer, a work of art exposes myths without breaking their spell of enchantment; likewise, as the scientist probes to the level of microbes and cells, the mystery of diseases may be solved but the awe at nature's creative power increases.

As I was completing my work, Hurricane Andrew devastated Fairchild Tropical Garden, blowing many of the trees and plants away. It was a lesson in the fragility of edenic dreams, a parallel to the winds of time that have blown away the words of the Book of Paradise. Yet the Hebraic heritage laid the groundwork for a Jewish tradition of renewal and metamorphosis that is text-centered, withstanding historical disasters. The creative talents in each generation were lifelong poets and scholars; in some periods these authors composed new books out of the commentaries of previous generations. The medieval Kabbalah, for instance, is full of lost, disguised, resurrected, and invented texts that parallel the Book of Paradise, including that major Jewish achievement, the *Zohar,* which makes a cornucopia out of catastrophe.

In the religion of Devorah Bat-David's time, conflict over the divine couple—in particular, the importance agriculture lent to fertility cults associated with the divine consort—was resolved in favor of a sexually repressed divinity of one. Yet the conflict persisted in the mystical tradition, flowering into great literary works at different periods. The greatest of these, Moses de León's *Zohar,* rivals in scope and poetics the dominant Christian work of the period, Dante's *Divine Comedy.* De León characterizes the female and male aspects of the creator as a divine couple in such sharp focus that the heavenly intercourse between them is the sustaining metaphor of the Jewish God: a nightly copulation that results in the creation of souls. (These heavenly souls, created male-female, split apart as they fall earthward.) While Dante can avoid the divine mother by beatifying an incarnate woman, de León must return to the source of Jewish creativity, the heavenly sexual conflict of the parental gods.

In the much earlier time of the Song of Solomon, the relations between divine lovers had been translated into earthly terms. Yet the energy of the great biblical poem derives from the earlier Book of Paradise, where the divine couple's sublimation into Adam and Eve was first accomplished. They are equals, even in the experience of sexual misadventure. Although these protagonists in Paradise have subjective thoughts, they are unable to contemplate rebellion; being godlike themselves, against whom would they revolt? Neither are Adam and Eve fully human enough to make passionate judgments about the world as speakers in later Hebraic poetry do, most notably in the biblical books of Psalms and Prophets.

I have presented Devorah Bat-David's editorial notations on the Book of Paradise in a contemporary idiom. In her age of the invention of poetic prose, the daring style she must have used is hard to approximate in a modern language, but it resembles parts of the Bible's books of Samuel written by the Solomonic court historian S, whose prose presaged the art of the novel.

In the process of imagining Devorah's work, I've occasionally appended my own notes to hers, following her example of brevity. She allows Adam, Eve, and the snakes to speak for themselves, just as the humans in Paradise allow the animals and plants to speak. In her reverence for the early Hebraic author lost in time, Devorah Bat-David displays more empathy for writers than her academic counterparts do today, whose control over the text is threatened by a poet's imaginative authority. The Adam given room to breathe by Devorah's scholarship is as dynamic as his or her author made him, free to yearn sexually and imaginatively for Eve. Instead of putting her own erudition in the way, Devorah lets us open the Book of Paradise directly upon Adam's passionate, intellectual search for a partner.

1075 B.C.E.

The Lost Book

of Paradise

CHAPTER 1

Because Adam is found in the midst of the Garden in the act of naming the plants, it is probable a prologue once existed that was erased from the surviving scroll. Yet perhaps no prologue was necessary, for it may have been the convention of the day to begin with Adam searching for his Eve among the creatures. However, here we first come upon Adam naming the plants in scenes that exist in no other archaic scroll, and I would venture that the work is inspired by the embrace of agriculture and horticulture, in a culture whose roots are in herding flocks and tending sheep.

Each naming is an encounter for Adam that foretells an intimacy for which he yearns. His naming power engenders a mission, a search for a mate who cannot be found because she has apparently not yet been created. Since this portion of the tale has not been tampered with by the old authorities, it is a unique aberration, a Hebraic twist of startling proportions, for no other scroll I have encountered in all the libraries of the East presents such a separate creation of Adam and Eve. We must therefore assume that the story of the gods, which the authorities removed before our scroll was copied or translated, depicted a creation for both Adam and Eve.

Nevertheless, the scroll adheres to the Hebraic tradition of a creation of the world out of words. Yet this particular old myth—that the plants and foods of Paradise are God's chosen medium between heaven and earth—is an archaic vestige of our culture, which has had a flourishing kingdom for ages and has been established for almost a hundred years. In this earlier time, when the tending of trees and orchards was a new development for Hebrews, the significance of horticulture may have seemed a source of liberating progress.

We can also see that in Genesis, particularly the J strand, Adam's stated purpose in the Garden—to watch and tend it—derives from usage of these verbs in the Book of Paradise. —D.R.

ADAM:
If I spoke to her in breaths
lips inspire lips
to press
to drink there
as all words swallowed like seeds
by the earth
to rest there, pregnant
waiting for their namer
as I for you, each naming
like your kiss, a pressing claim
to memory: alone,

Paradise has no mirror
in intimate eyes, though
all living things talk
ask me their name
and regard me for finding Adam in earth
sweet savor of death there turned into life
grass eaten and growing again
sleep the wine the ovum suckles
the seeds of plant-bodies still virgin
with expectation of knowing everything
themselves, their names
their bodies run to the sun, grow and grow
as their watcher awakes, earth, myself.

CHAPTER 2

In another passage of naming, Adam becomes aware of his loneliness, longing to identify with his mate and not have to learn by mistakes. As there is no congress among animals in Paradise, how might Adam come to speak of offspring? We must bear in mind that he has become familiar with reproduction from tending the plants; these produce all the food he and all the creatures will ever need.

The naming of the sheep must have had special significance for this nation of shepherds. The convention of an Adam incapable of seeing himself and hence capable of mistaking any creature for his mate, while far from our notions of moral supremacy over nature, is here raised nevertheless to a tragic dimension. In his isolation Adam views himself as treelike, aligning himself with the noble purpose of the trees of knowledge and life, deriving once again from the ancient Hebraic embrace of horticulture.

Adam's naming power is dramatized by a passionate empathy with each animal and plant; his drive to find his partner is a representation of his creative force. Adam's creative powers are clearly dependent on his fearless atti-

*tude toward making mistakes. In modern terms, we might
say that Adam embodies the evolutionary principle of diversity, where each species approaches every changing condition by striving to colonize it—thus changing themselves—
ultimately to inhabit the widest range of environments.
—*D.R.

ADAM:
Her bone must be mine, as if I was taken
out of her—or her of me
she might be offspring
the way the bones announce themselves through the head
unbranched and never shed
when I covered myself in her fleece she bolted
then stopped, waiting for me
I was almost insulted but as I hugged her again
it was even better—I must lose her
I said to myself, and persist, finding—
without me she too is lost, my mate
then the bigger one appeared, bones
coiled atop like trumpets to call her
were she strayed even up a mountain.
I learned—as I named them fondly, sheep—
my mate would share my fear
that our hearts might stray though prove
loyal in turning back, catching up
with the other's numb silence
as if the coiled organ of my heart
called out—in her I look for the limits
of myself: tension
where the air starts, a dropping off

surrounding us: all that is in me
is in the Garden
I'll know it all to know her
be lost to find her
no skin to burrow my nose in
no flank to chew with tender bites
no silhouette to shape my gaze
and close my eyes, my ears
caressed by her heart's growl
lost, it's a worse death not to touch
the tree of myself, rooted and branched
in all angles playing for light
and she hides from me, my skin of leaves
my bones of fruit
my home is spirit walking
on the afternoon breezes: the breath of God
on my neck, calming
as I watch shadows breathe also
and recede, like beings.

CHAPTER 3

In this chapter employing two voices, Adam first imagines Eve's voice, using a contemporary idiom as a device to indicate she is a character in his dream. While Eve's voice is heard as an observer of Adam, she has not been created yet. Many of the ancient paradise scrolls employ dreams exclusively, and these observations of Adam are his own, expressing the loneliness he feels. Then, in a complementary passage, Adam speaks as he names the creature seen in the dream of Eve.

EVE:
When their watcher, Adam, stirs
all stir as I would
were I then but black rock
perhaps in a swoon he will fall upon me
hug tight to my back and thighs
as if stone sculpted into black bear
for him I would be black tar
on the royal road of my king—
tethered to midnight, a sun worshiper who cringes
at his withdrawal in winter, who curls up and hides
in a den and lies motionless for long months.

ADAM:
Now the nose scents dark warmth
a steam of fur so rich
black to the mind as gold in the ore
and I hear the bending grass before her
she moves massively as I do when called by a thought
in my mind, as if her shadow
as if thought bending before it, my being a blade of grass
now she steps from the trees in black splendor
walking on each flat foot (is there a tail?)
ears match my hand; in her mouth, pears and grapes
I bury my head in her hind leg and smell deep to her skin
fruit trees in autumn, fur the mulching ground
I climb her back, my head falls over hers
as legs straddle belly
nose over nose I moisten my face
inhale her fruity breath, honey-dipped.

CHAPTER 4

Adam's naming all living things in the Garden continues, as this chapter develops his relationship to the trees and plants, here to an ancient palm tree. Adam embraces it as a living form that also represents his potential mate. The Canaanitish background of sacred tree worship is probably at work here, although it was also a convention in Egyptian culture to depict scholars under palm trees.

This association between trees and scholarship may be a fundamental and crucial development in Hebraic culture. The long Jewish tradition of diverse commentary, with one book metamorphosing into another in a later age, parallels the ancient Greek notion of art imitating nature. New fruit, like new books, points to the importance of memory. Again, Adam as tender of the Garden must learn from the plants and allow them to reproduce, just as a diverse tradition of commentary nurtures Hebraic culture. Devorah's ancient commentary serves as illustration. —D.R.

ADAM:
Take this palm that ravishes me, uncoiling
an articulate head, wild

like a scholar's, she speaks
directly to my thoughts, bypassing sound—
as light outlines a tree, colors and shapes it
so words do thought
leaves each a feather of a finger
pleated into a fan: a tribe
of mothering breezes
or any plant or thing I've named—
but clear as sound in darkness she speaks
hair a gossip's running voice
turning into an infant's sweet babbling
as I rest my nose on the breeze there
voice becoming a wise entertainer
fingers caressing my ear:
these are leaves teaching me care
to open my lips boldly
accept the milk of the nut—
evangelist of sweet things, I say
go-between, coconut.

CHAPTER 5

Eve's voice is heard in dream again, observing Adam as in Chapter 3. Again, this device helps portray Adam in his loneliness as he searches for his mate. Although it may appear humorous to us, in fact this chapter makes use of the ancient Egyptian catalog of animals, where they are described in human terms. The writer seems to draw as well upon an older tradition of animal fables.

I must note the strong likelihood that the author is building upon old myths we have forgotten, where gods spoke in animal form and cohabited with humans.

Devorah's literary intuition is accurate. This chapter seems to be an anxiety dream as Adam is obsessed with his naming. Further, Devorah's attempt to characterize the author's sources is authentic. There were no doubt many scrolls from cultures as far away as India in the Phoenician and Philistine libraries, chronicling the interactions of men, animals, and gods. —D.R.

EVE:
Now look: one flies to him, her hand
a wing of skin, the thumb clawing free

a leaflike structure in enlarged ear
an inflected bounce
from Adam's eye to her huger one
a voice clicking her words in the dark
I've seen you in the afternoon, says Adam, hanging
among leaves, head straight down
Call me, she says, am I yours?
He strokes a furry face, a velvet
to his bristling beard—it softens him
the blood in him thickening as he licks
the inside of her silken wing
holding her legs in each hand like teats
Is this mine, he sighs, are you lone
but she squeaks softly: one clicks
to my heart, hanging in the trees,
I hear him batting the fruit.

CHAPTER 6

Adam forms the first question as he searches for his mate. The voice of Adam here is built upon the Canaanitish poems about sacred groves I found in the Joppa library. A man would go to the groves to ask a question and receive an oracle from the priests. Yet here Adam expresses his isolation from Eve as a question about his purpose in the Garden, for the first time linking his mission to tend the Garden with the necessity of his search for a mate.

My question here is where was Yahweh? Can it be that Yahweh withdrew from his creation, seeing that the creature in his own image cannot be independent of his mate, as Yahweh intended? In the same way, we will find that the angels have withdrawn into the flowers and the demons into winds. Although Yahweh will return to create Eve, he is not present in the story.

More probable, however, is that Yahweh's presence was removed by the old scribes, since the scroll may have included what they would have deemed crude details about Yahweh's interactions with his creatures or, even worse to their ears, a description of his relations with his own consort, the Shekhinah.

There is presumably an echo of this in Adam's naming of the bush.

In this archaic time, when the tending of orchards was a new development for Hebrews, the mysteries revealed must have seemed a liberating progress to the scroll's writer.

ADAM:

Searching for what? The question
falls like leaves, like seeds and what else
blowing in fall
all seasons here at once: green the tree
remains, snow at her foot, fruit
a rainbow blur on her
and then the blazing leaves forming a question
where was she
and as I fall to thought I find my bed
the ground that is me, Adam
from there always rising
up like tree sap
till it outruns the tree itself
reaching herself for fulfilling sun—
reaching fills me, and so the fall, the question
spread out like a brilliant explosion
on the ground, as if a god had plummeted
his words bright leaves and somber cones
husks of a long interrogation
but where would I begin
as I began, mouthing these words
sun my blanket
night the bed on which I sang

creating—to go on without end is proof
of what I can't make, another
an end to turn me
to fall on me like the ground
rising again in the stirrups of my hands
until I too explode, but upwards like the cedars
the blood of wild grapevine in fall
wrapped blazing around my trunk
bursting memory
leaving lasting fragrance, lasting wood
my own garden
but where is she—with only hard wood
in my hands, unpresented
to my flower of flowers
enclosed in her soft skin
as on this bush reaching to my waist
her long climbing arms veiled in little hooks
I reach my hand in to the lower leaves, grasping
one, its five leaflets, turned in my handshake
to their lower, lighter green surface
less coarse there, yet nothing to prepare
for the skin as if of an inner organ
that is each red flower
bearing small oval fruits like tongues
caressing my ear as if it were in a cradle
a body's cradle—hips I call them
as they first cup the rose
moist texture that bids my blood
rise. The bones cradle
wet warmth a nose likewise senses
a rose, in bud or flower, the eyes

delve to that secret—closed, seeing
through hand and mouth, silent tongue
searching the cradle of lips
until everything heard becomes breathing.

CHAPTER 7

This chapter begins with Adam naming a feline. When he realizes she is not his mate he is confronted with the snake. All animals come to Adam to hear their names pronounced, but the snake has found a way to be deposited at his feet, thus surprising Adam.

The snake is not supernatural as in some tales but supremely natural, the subtlest of the creatures. She is also the most sensual and in Paradise appears to be the happiest of creatures. For happiness in the Garden entails a delight in perfection, which is reflected in the command of oneself and the manner in which each limb and each organ is alert to its fulfillment. The female snake is the same Lilith in some archaic Canaanitish scrolls, but I also found a likeness in Sanskrit and Indo-Tamil scrolls, proving that the author was learned in languages and had visited many libraries.

As Adam feels Lilith become a part of himself, he confuses her with Eve through what he has learned about seduction from tending the Garden. This is a distinctly Hebraic Lilith, who does not so much seduce Adam as allow him to be seduced by his own

wishes. We find traditional tales of other Hebraic
women in similar circumstances, especially the tale
of Tamar, who disguises herself as Judah's prostitute.

*Absorbed in naming, Adam experiences an intimacy with
living things that is based on identification: to know and
name it, Adam identifies with each. The intimacy is never
a true sharing, as Adam only wishes to identify himself
through finding his mate. But there is already the hint of
deeper need from the loneliness engendered by the search.*

 *Lilith's ability to seduce reminds Adam that his powers
of language are also seductive, since they reproduce images, and presumably this is what he has learned from
tending plants: each flowers in order to seduce an animal
to carry its pollen.* —D.R.

ADAM:
Her tongue washing my face
pupils a jeweled slit in the light
I am lost in the hood of her ear
as she hears herself—tenses
and I return to the tail, frozen upright now
she bolts then creeps back to rub
a scent on my tailbone with her head
I want to charm she purrs
deposits snake at my feet—no, I am less mercurial
I thought though my back arched like hers
as snake uncoiled up to my eyes between us
and filled up her size
What a fine skull, I thought, with openings
coupled behind each eye socket, subtle and deep

taking in everything as I am wrapped also
in sound vibrating in my bones
resonating to the snake's hearing bone—
she hears first, it seems, and I only follow
like a horse its master
or its master, Pharaoh
"To the water," she whispers, "to look at thyself"
There, I see only the animal
who lives on the surface, like dust
and mimics me (I cannot hear his water voice)
whose mate I've yet to see
"Where is the mate?" I ask the snake standing at my shoulder
I met the eye of this creature unnamed
who peers through lenses
as though I was far away, her mouth too
opens so largely when she speaks
the soft sound surprises
and the flicked forked tongue
withdrawn as if she was sipping air
to taste it—my scent there
but how can I know it?—an odorless mirror
of this elegantly folded skin
scale against scale in perfect place
a sack whose mouth is rightly around her lips
the skin loosened there, as she talks, moving
as her body moves—serpentine I call it—a wave of muscles
rippling down each side of her body
that excites me too, my skin quivering—
it's like my own thought, shimmering
a reflection of—the light the plants face
as the animals turn away, all

I've seen, save this snake
her voice in my head
excites me while it curves around thoughts
like light around the dazzling fruits
the voice like light I cannot face, to know
its source by description, by naming
only the plants can impart this
as they seduce me in every shape
fruit, nut, flower, leaf, branch and bole
each with two names: its own and granting another
invisible, the seed within
my thoughts the seeds the plants impart
as they teach us to eat them
and spread their seed
and plant them male and female, multiplying
to feed us, while we are multiplied
merely with words of gratitude: description
and longing for knowing what's within
by desire to praise its outer shape: a mate
and all that might resemble her.

CHAPTER 8

Eve was created while Adam slept, the creator belat-
edly putting an image of his female partner into
Paradise. A priest might call God's consort his feminine side. Eve proceeded to identify her mate in the
same way Adam did, mistaking him in the male
snake, Samael. The creator could not create Eve with
a revealed purpose because he had left unrevealed the
hidden presence in the Garden of his female partner.
Thus the first mistake made by Eve was natural and
inevitable.

Although the characters of Samael and Lilith are
very old Hebraic myth, our writers today portray
them with subtlety, as spirits who inhabit the snakes,
and not the male and female creatures themselves.
Here they are natural snakes, created as subtle climb-
ers.

Already Eve is considering not only her relation
to her mate but to her creator or parent. When Adam
eventually finds her, he will experience the mother
in Eve as well as the mate.

*Eve is endowed like Adam with the power of naming. In
all the Hebraic creation tales we sense the creator's need for*

intimacy, sublimated into a lonely Adam. Why is the creator avoiding intimacy in heaven? Eve too had the naming power, which is the god-given sublimation of intimacy, a need to share. The creator himself created by naming the world into existence.

Common to creator and Adam and Eve is the creative principle necessary for naming—a principle none of the other creatures possess. This creative principle allows for the mistaking of identities. For Adam and Eve, the need to defend against mistakes will lead to intimacy, sharing, marriage, for they can't trust themselves without a partner.

Mistakes in the Garden are sexual, as is the nectar-producing reproduction of plants and the language of naming, which Adam and Eve learn from the reproducing of fruits. So the pride and self-reliance that reflect their maker also has to submit to sexuality, the same process their creator—reproducing his image—sublimated in himself, leading to his loss of divine consort, who disguises herself in the sacred tree. Without the first couple's mistakes in Paradise, leading to sublimation and intimacy, there could have been no creative principle.

This interpretation of the plot in the Book of Paradise shows it to be a harbinger of modern science. Evolutionary selection suggests that a drive for independence or distance from parent species in plants helped them to colonize new earth, and the diversity of these "mistakes" bred new species.   —D.R.

EVE:
I woke up under flowers
Where was he?

murmuring water
drew me; smooth as another sky
this river, and by it I dreamed
my first dream, and heard
my mate, answering my question
your form awakes my desire;
alone, you were my dream
Adam has my desire even when I am not there
he holds my place
and I his: arms and legs moving
to enfold each other, one ambition
rooted as trees—those
holding the center of the Garden
their flowers a world of faces
and behind them, nectar-consciousness
I must have drunk to wake
to know when I dream in this rooted place
words my faces and flowers
the word-roots ambrosia
no sooner tasted than seen—
I am no spirit but implanted
in this body: only by the knowledge I eat
can I outreach these hands, see
into myself and find
the rose of Sharon and the lily of the Valleys
and all are Eve: I create her
my mind races to distances beyond
an angel's—return, return
and no goddess returns. I may look all ways—
no god may blind me
no king, no queen of heaven

Yet rooted within is a name held back
as if my heart overtook my man's desire
mother—to name all I take in, hidden.

CHAPTER 9

Why were the snakes given power to climb into the
tree of knowledge? It must be remarked that in many
paradise scrolls there is ambivalence about the consort God as well as the source of childbirth. In the
Hebraic tale, the Shekhinah is recognizable as the
tree of knowledge. Why would God plant it there
and leave it so vulnerable? We can only guess that
the Shekhinah was somehow involved and that her
power also directed God's hand in creating the snake
and then the man in his image.

SAMAEL:
"Taste and see," he said, "the fruit
I climbed the height of my being to attain
pulled toward my goddess: heartbreaking,
my sister, are thy sculpted feet
bearing your full weight whether you come or go
each thigh like milk, liquid marble
a work of passion
the tender orifice between brimming
thy breasts twin fawns
stopping there
altogether a statuesque palm, my dear

breasts each a cluster of dates
I said, I will go up to the high one
grasp the highest fruit for this love
as I would take hold of thy boughs
the smell of thy nose like mangoes
roof of thy mouth the finest aroma
of wine that goes down sweetly
fragrant bunches of grapes thy breasts."

CHAPTER 10

As the creator was obliged to create Eve, it seems also he was obliged to place the food of the gods in the Garden, in the form of the Shekhinah's tree of knowledge. Here already was the question in Paradise, the presence of godly fruit but the hidden wisdom of the Shekhinah.

EVE:
Your tongue occupies me
I am planted, cannot move
what more like gods than trees
no partner missed, no need
of another: a gift to all
a giving no words limit
flowers to share each breath
the tree I might call father
so tall it takes my breath away
as I look up its exquisite bulk
it is unattainable, no branch within reach
limbs of pendant fruit like a large male
beckoning my tiny hand
should I not want to wrap myself in his skin?
appetite has pulled me heavenward

toward your mouth, curving
to entwine with mine
incoherent in the mirror of his subtlety
his head swaying as he sang
I clutched him there, my mouth opened
I swam in the highest fruit
vowed singing and tending
to that precious tree, ease to her
fertile burden as I grew weighty—
"I would return," I said to myself.

CHAPTER 11

The scroll now returns to Lilith and Adam in their part of the Garden. The author will keep both mis-conceiving couples before us, to emphasize how they were created separately and thus to miss each other.

Adam begins to learn the Garden of Eden's origin from Lilith, who like her mate Samael has eaten from Wisdom's tree.

LILITH:
I must answer my master of names
with all I have learned from eating
all food is knowledge
of where we have been, origin
of distinction, character-builder, joiner
of senses to hidden nutriment, namer of wisdom
You ask: "And if this tree of knowledge
is also my creator, is the mother
who would have me, known by her absence?"
He didn't want you to know, wanted you
his own reflection in earth, hidden from her
The God put his queen behind you
and I feel the power of her secret
when you welcome me nakedly

as he must feel her reserve
it is almost too much, her limits
turn pride to yearning—for what?
how to be absent and present
and then to know more: to burst into knowledge
as if thoughts were seeds
to be Her: dominate the earth, watch
as life listens for your naming voice
causing me to hear
nothing is more fair than thou, my dove's eyes
my hair of mountain goat, rare
my sheep's pearl teeth, shorn and washed
each one with its twin, above and below
thy lips as dawn's first scarlet
temples shining like pomegranates through the leaves
that are your head's golden strands
neck a towering palm laden with a thousand
pounds of fruit I gaze upon
from a mountain
from the lions' den, from the leopards' lair
from within my knowing heart, my man
She, thy mothering knowledge, would have you eat
her tree made tall for climbing
not for gazing upon
and so I have mounted and sucked
the fruit eaten
to know all that is here:
all is here, even the gods
who have climbed out of their forms
to reproduce and be smelled
touched, tasted, seen—

fragrant flower, textured leaf
sweet seed capsule, bursting color
sentient texts in love with the air
and bodies that rub against them
birds that have heard their song
coursing through the veins of living things
opening all mouths
silent themselves as great opened books
with all the seductive powers words dryly mimic—
the names you give enclose stale air
but their documents of cells breathe life
still you may hear new music
in each limitation, each bound name
for it will propagate a thing
in the mind, sing
to you as you climb
out of your body, into mine.

CHAPTER 12

Now Adam dreams Eve's voice again. He dreams her as if she has already tasted the fruit, as if she were Lilith and justifying his desire to know her. For Adam has not yet eaten and so has not yet acquired an inner life of thought, a secret life.

Devorah might suggest in our day, with the benefit of Freud, that Eve is shown becoming aware of her unconscious—of an inner realm that leaves her in exile from Adam. When Adam will bite into this knowledge himself, he will hear Eve's voice within himself just as if it were his own, for they are perfectly matched.   —D.R.

EVE:
How could you see, my man
how insubstantial the food of knowledge
except to the mouth, an invisible
thinking, a climbing into thought, not out
not into another—this food of gods
grown from a greater thinking
as were we, created
to contain our own seed, a companion
mistook in another subtle face

inhabited by godly thoughts: both ourselves
and their serpent bodies sated—
to make creation endless
in a head endlessly thinking
how to praise its glorious mate
each breath a word of praise.

The Lost
Book of
Paradise

CHAPTER 13

Returning to Samael and Eve, the male snake explains how Adam was created to search for Eve in his loneliness. The snake's acquired knowledge lends him the majesty that Eve continues to mistake for her mate. Having eaten from the food of the gods, Samael has divined Eve's origin in the Shekhinah's desire to embody her place in Paradise. As Samael tells the story of her origin as well as the origin of Paradise, he seduces her with wisdom.

The account of the plants in the Garden is unlike any I have found in the libraries. Perhaps this knowledge of gardening has already been lost to us.

A rudimentary understanding of pollination is glimpsed here, and even a crude foretaste of knowledge about evolution. This period was a brief forerunner—as Akhenaton's reign in Egypt foretold monotheism—of later science. This should not be surprising, since we find similar instances in Ancient Greek thought, and some archaic translations of the latter, perhaps dating back to Sumer, would have been available in the Phoenician libraries of the ancient Middle East. —D.R.

SAMAEL:
The more Adam joyed, embracing and naming
all creation as God would
the more he felt you were lost
almost lost: there is no loss
in Paradise that is not found
in the next moment—one moment is all
there is, or two moments: all is coupled
nothing or something, dark and light
inside and out—now
and then. Then, there was She
in heaven, and now there is her tree
this one knowledge, good and bad
mated to his one, life—
so he must promise Adam an Eve
or Adam himself learns a third thing
a thing forever lost, an eternity
and climb up, as I have climbed
to leave this body
and be with gods. Yet bodiless angels
think it best here, embodied
as flowers, speaking in senses
but leaving silence for words to grow
seeds of flower speech, persuading
another to approach
not to be restlessly always persuading
leaving a seductive bouquet
but in another moment
what is now open will become
the secret, what joys always
will become moments

the house of the world
will become a small house
even a room, a
bed, a body itself
housing the secret world
shot through
with love because everything
the whole world again
is for telling, the first words
like green figs the tree puts forth
and the smell of tender grapes
ripened on the vine
arise, if I am your love.

CHAPTER 14

Eve has understood the congress Samael requests. This notion of congress is similar to that of gods and angels in many of the older epics and tales, where the entities melt into one another.

Here too we see Eve naming Adam, complementing his powers.

With this speech Eve begins to realize she is a sublimation of the female divine—or the feminine aspect of it. —D.R.

EVE:
But why don't I know what to say?
You have taught me another speech
you open me like a seed
before I can think, these words too opening
as if planted in the earth: *Adam,*
I name you
to hold you against the dissolving
wind, healing the rift in it
in which you see our history, sublimity
to see what is there by looking at air
as you show me the creator's partner
and I embrace her on my own tongue

we all must be one
created in place of her
so I take that place for you
my earth, to be your water
though we are neither
and words are merely reproducing
what has brought us here: new bodies
the language of eternity (as you have shown)
known by the god-trees—ruled voiceless to me.

CHAPTER 15

As I have iterated, horticulture was a new culture for
the Hebrews at this time. Tropical fruits from Africa
and the East were introduced by caravans, opening
the mind to the plant world's diversity. I have read
where the textures of many meats, spicy and pun-
gent, are reproduced in the odd-shaped fruits from
the tropics, revealing far more in fruit than a familiar
storehouse of sweets. And thereby, no doubt, the
myth of all foods present in the Garden was realized.

   The close association between knowledge and sexual congress is attested to, just as in the relationship
between knowledge and the natural world. As we
shall see later, in the description of a timeless Paradise where everything returns when it is recognized,
Samael in his subtlety imparts the paradisiacal view
of loss as renewal, as the trees teach.

SAMAEL:
To name them—ruling tree couple
of the Garden—embodies each:
Knowledge, of good and bad
is partner to our creator's Life
though good and bad are split apart

cannot be brought together knowingly
yet here in Paradise the plants alone express
a desire to move beyond and everywhere
to outgrow the knowledge
with life itself—so much
do angels hunger to create worlds
in their master's image, each flower
learning the skill of life from animals
buzzing with talk from their drink
and vegetable meal: a diversity of tastes
enlarging memory and the chances
to recognize loss in something new
and to swallow it honeyed, eating it whole
each part of the plant on a palette
eyed to taste, down to the inner flame of carrot
at the root—leaf a spinach emerald
bud pearl-nippled, a cauliflower
the ovary a pear that is you, my dear
distilled into smooth liqueur
and from all this a bliss of mistakes
endless resemblances to learn from.

CHAPTER 16

The congress of Eve and Samael is seen from Eve's eyes, holding to her imagined Adam as to a brother, compounding the tragedy of error. Yet there is no tragedy to this text, only change and transformation, as we find common among Hebraic scrolls. Today we think of renewal as almost a standard Hebraic theme, although we have developed a tragic dimension by imposing categories of right and wrong and responsibility.

Samael alludes to his unnatural congress with Eve by using the same terms for broken boundaries as we find in Yahweh's speech to Moses in the new historic scroll. But it appears to be brilliant wordplay without serious responsibility, indeed a paradise.

I would add that the theme of the abandoned lover is quite common in the Indian scrolls we have recently acquired for Solomon's palace library. In them, the male lover embarks on long caravan journeys to see the world, as his female companion is left to yearn.

It is worth noting that, in Solomon's Song, much of this chapter is absorbed into a portrayal of Solomon's relations with the Queen of Sheba, whom he loved but was pressed to abandon by the entire court.

*Devorah here provides evidence for the uncanny metamor-
phosis of Hebraic poems and narratives—we see how natural it was for ancient readers to expect such continuity.*
—D.R.

6 2

*The Lost
Book of
Paradise*

E V E :
I slept but my heart was awake
open to me, my brother, my gate
my undivided mate
conjoined we are one word, union
each to conjugate there
new language, reproduce—
no food more than thy lips as they part
no wine more than thy heart cups
"Come, beloved, let us go
into the field" I heard myself say
"under his tree
so we please our father
bound not to touch him except by the eyes"
My man who coiled inside me
whom I held firmly
whose hand was on the lock of my being
pulled it away—
I awoke and
a softness spread in me
I was drawn to him
open within
and then I was desolate and empty
my heart leapt from my breast
my hands were drenched, as if with perfume—
I alone was open to him

but my feet were a statue's feet
lifeless clay, naked earth
"What is wrong?" I asked my man
and the snake replied, "Love
is breaking bounds
But you will sing like a skylark
like the angels whose voices are withdrawn
into faces of flowers
giving sweet nectar to the singers
that wake their mouths to words
all language is the mating of angels
good and bad—the bad who fell
are the winds who taught
singing."

CHAPTER 17

Eve will hear that Samael is not her mate. This news quickens her thirst for knowledge, and the consequence of eating the tree's fruit seems negligible. In the new court history by our contemporary, the fruit takes on a higher moral value.

It is with difficulty that I understand the similarity here depicted between a thirst for congress and for knowledge. It is not easy to grasp the impiety of sexual congress that was tolerated here. However, we must grant the charm of this primitive attitude as it is depicted. Perhaps there are remnants of supernatural fables no longer familiar to us. If so, they are no doubt Hebraicized, since the power of the gods is diminished while Yahweh's power is not yet enlarged upon.

SAMAEL:
Thy words, fair one, are a liquid gold
I will remember your love
more precious than any draught
there is no blot on you, no stain from within
the smell of your skin drowns out all spices
honey and milk are under your tongue

I will come into my garden, my sister
But I am not your man
though inward man, as I have also eaten
as one before me: Lilith, my mate
I saw her die and live again inward woman
as your eyes have opened to a mother
see: I am the male snake
you have given me knowledge
by your tongue, so I may lead you
to your tongue's mate, the man
who named me so I might grow
whole in all subtle chances
I've united you with your parent tree
from whom I ate and you
through me will: I'll climb
again for you.

CHAPTER 18

Now the congress and comprehension of her mistake further stimulate the thirst for knowledge in Eve. This thirst calls forth memory and a desire to satisfy it, to know origins. The knowledge that is reserved for gods, we learn, is about origins and the power of creation.

We have progressed to an understanding of our origins in historical dimensions today and are distrustful of myth. Yet even in this scroll we must assume that much from the fantastic realm has been withdrawn. Instead, we are presented a quasi-natural tale that owes a good deal to the recent knowledge of horticulture. The author of this scroll, however, was likely to have satirized the myths of the time pertaining to sacred tree worship.

The snakes, like all other creatures, did not have the interpretive imagination we humans were given—our "naming" power—which allowed us to learn the language of reproducing images from trees, according to the Book of Paradise. Only we could use this power to create our own gardens—or to destroy them. —D.R.

SAMAEL:
Where have you come from
and how were you made?
I will tell you all
I have seen. Here before your man
was created, I saw the trees
colonizing the ground, air
I saw the angels disappear—into the ground
lacking sensible bodies
and they are here now, returning as flowers
I saw the demons disappear into the air
to come back disembodied wind—
creatures do not listen to them
but drink from the flowers and learn
to speak; from nectar I acquired
these words with which you were born
to feed the spirits
with stories of our lives here, to entice them
to our bodies with flowers described
and when they attend us we summon their meal
from the spirit within us, the dream
to quench them in the river of language
a flow of reproducing images or seeds
to be eaten when embedded in tales
and dropped into our Garden when we wake
to tell them. This whole story I tell
I saw as in a dream. We all, the creatures
tended the plants teaching us to speak.
Two great trees in the midst of the Garden
were planted before you came
their fruits so high I feared the climb:

parents, your food
for knowing the gods, whose image of food they bear
your roots, for they ruled here before you.

CHAPTER 19

The tale of naturalistic origins in the Garden continues.

SAMAEL:
Now the angels longed for bodies in Eden
as seeds are in passion to burst the ground
speaking in a rainbow of tongues
fruit asks to be eaten
by the farthest flying animal
to let the seeds pass through
fall to the ground far from harm
threatening a group enghettoed
or hidden away and forgotten by squirrels
there's no end to the clothes they wear
organic wraps (jacket husks
to silken skins)
burrs grasp the fastest thing
or float away on thistly parachutes
The man also longed to see his seed
after he swallowed the godseed
as Eve had, wanting him
to join with her and leave
God's Garden, make their own

where time reigned and seasons
fell apart, one following the next
the light grew and withdrew, rain
dropped when all things trembled for it
Once man was free, time was his
to dance, to display, to court
until he fell off his feet, unbalanced
having no mate to bear him
to melt at his call—he longed to yell
with a joy that matches a child's wail.

CHAPTER 20

Although Samael appears to have anticipated it, Adam has not yet eaten. Lilith answers Adam as Samael answered Eve, explaining the origins that can satisfy Adam's sense of what is missing. Employing Adam's experience in naming but one thing at a time to the exclusion of others, Lilith explains how memory is selective. Therefore, Adam must tend his memory and thoughts in the same way he tended the Garden of Eden itself.

Lilith becomes almost demonic in her revelation of food and eating as knowledge of parentage and the gods. It is as if she is intoxicated with knowledge. How can Adam believe her? The news he is hearing must also drive him to eat.

LILITH:
A mind focuses like a bird's eye
picking out only what it needs
to feed upon: red, orange, yellow
bursting quietly out of green, turning
itself from unripened green—like a thought
of resistance among general calm
A mind ignores the backdrop world

paints it out
with a broad brush of serenity
leaving its tiny fire totally to infuse
one bright concept—
such was man created
in God's latest image, focused
to a point of brilliance
against a heaven of tranquil pearl
when he was set gemlike in the Garden
that womb once free from *oneness*
among the forerunning plants
that feed from first light of creation
to create the jewelry of endless fruits
sheltering there the stellar parents of life
male and female, the two trees
manifesting food of the gods
their fruits softly glowing
as if from another world
All this I know from climbing
the great tree, persuaded to eat
and here I heard the past
that there was a thing lost, a past
that could not be found in the Garden
unlike all else that always returns
soon as it is recognized. In heaven
God knows his She and planted
a Garden for her
Wisdom is her tree, as Life
is his—both bear fruit
for gods. Why are you here
if not to be the image of God

to eat the food of his thought?
As I in Wisdom's image
learned we eat embodiments
in Eden, offspring of godly thoughts
enticed into being by his angels
softly seducing the animals
to spread their angelic bloom
and this divine food is further stirred
by the voices of demons in the wind
restrained from returning to the Garden
for when they were here
they craved form and entered the trees
but now they howl outside
songless
Yet here you are, himself
and you have found your queen
a bee has come to the rose
sit down under my shadow
sweet my fruit to thee
rise up, my love, to me.

C H A P T E R   2 1

When Adam learns, presumably after their congress, that Lilith is not his mate he experiences a sharper loneliness, the mistake in his creation. More is missing than Eve, he thinks, as he acquires his own idea of a Garden. He now conceives that he may learn from his mistakes; Adam requires an intimacy that was not planned for him.

Beyond intimacy, Adam bodied forth an all-inclusiveness like his creator, so his blemish is a reflection. Needing to re-create himself, Adam prepares to eat the Borassus fruit, from the ancestral tree. In so doing he parallels Eve's earlier experience of inwardness.

Borassus palm is the species that many botanists believe is the prototype in paradise stories. The animals are free because they have their identifying reflections for mates as Adam depicts their happiness—they are free, that is, of his interior need for intimacy as he tries to depict his own happiness. —D.R.

ADAM:
A Garden where she is undiscovered
I can't name

I hear myself in the silence of trees
when the wind dies and they can't move
except to grow, only upward—
unlike animals—to drop our food
I listen in between the wind, Eve's whispering
and grow inside, looking
into the world again with her eyes
she makes me a part of her, apart
and partner—to the trees;
the animals have their mates outside;
reflection found, they eat freely and listen
for fruit to drop, for nectar brimming
excitement sings them to sleep
the rivers run to the same seductive tune
and the fish are steered to the plants there
Many tongues speak in the night
as some trees open their enticing white stars
drawing the moth and bat
and the glowing worm outlines the path
my thoughts also flower as I lie on the grass
gaze upward into their shining blossoms
painted on canvas unfurling in black
those stars unfold a fiction in me
wheeling harmonies for my dreams
tied to the crickets' beating feet
inhaling the night skin's cool fragrance
To close my eyes on a day's wonder
I anticipate Eve, illumined
in the bright branches of my thought
you taste me, bite deep
into me: the joy a death blow
to my attention, my body waking instead

wants to find you and invent
itself in your image
to feel I was created and know
my limit in yours, the bottom
in which I can press no farther
rooted as the colossal palm—
not he nor his mate but their fruit
comes closest to me
tasting you in the marrow
my teeth surprised to sink
deeper than my mouth could move—locked
in solid milk
silent
listening to your subtle winds.

CHAPTER 22

Now we see the effects on Adam of his congress with
Lilith, although he does not yet know of his mistake.
He hears an inward voice, desires secrecy, and thirsts
for knowledge of his creator.

ADAM:
I hear a voice that is mine
and then another—and as I do
the first voice wavers
my father must have two voices
one that I have not heard
Does he long for mine that speaks
in secret, as if to Eve
as I for his other utterance?
Do I have a mother?
I have heard a voice like the mountain dove's
full as a mouthful of snow
I would know her face as if my own
that is reflected in every dear appearance
even beneath a defying translucence
that is Lilith's smoky aspect
for my snake spoke of the maternal
tree; as she climbed for the fruit

the leaves trembled so tenderly
my mouth opened of its own accord
as if speaking.

CHAPTER 23

Now that Adam will learn his origins from the trees, he contemplates eating the fruit of the tree of knowing good and bad, as it is called in our contemporary's new history. But Adam first rejects the idea, appearing to express the old prohibition against incest.

The ancestor trees to which Adam refers remind us again of the tree worship in our past, as well as a cult of earth worship that is reflected in Adam's words.

Devorah's comment might suggest ancient intimation about the Darwinian speculation borne out by contemporary biology, in which the first habitat of our prehuman ancestors probably was in the trees, specifically the canopies of rain forests. —D.R.

ADAM:
The more I eat
the more I lose by forgetting
more hungry to taste and see
and feel my way toward her
then know the earth I'm made from

the two ancestral trees
one of respect for life
untouched, the other grasped only by forgetting
that it is untouchable
touching it, I would be lost
losing the memory
of my source, water and root
a mother fully in relation to herself
a father breaking the bond
to life going on forever
they are the parents of all I eat
sustaining me
in each moment my mouth, nostrils open.

CHAPTER 24

Adam now becomes aware that part of himself is as if already outside the Garden, for he finds hidden in the Garden a correspondence to his own secret. That parallel is the Shekhinah, representing the wisdom to reproduce, and she is discovered through his mistake. Corresponding to Adam's sense of an outside world, ancient cultures knew of other worlds of awareness, in trance and dream; and in our contemporary's new history, we find that Adam was put into such a trance by Yahweh in order to create Eve.

Yet Adam also learns that his task of tending the Garden entails learning how language, reproduction, and above all seduction, which is responsible for mistakes, are natural. He finds in this knowledge an expression of his own inwardness. His origins, then, can be divined from the trees.

It is difficult to penetrate the scroll's mystery here, for it seems to suggest that God intended for Adam to learn the truth about himself from tending the Garden that God also created. Perhaps it is the Shekhinah who is responsible for the knowledge in nature, although we do not know what happened in heaven that caused this result. Nevertheless, it was common in most archaic myths to render nature as a primary mother. Only in the Book of Paradise, however, is nature rendered as heavenly wisdom. I must assume this is some archaic mystery, especially as Adam interprets the plants to be inhabited by spirits, in the same manner that the snakes had earlier explained the presence of angels.

How interesting that Devorah interprets Adam's sense of another world, for it is as if she is describing the unconscious. She seems to avoid here the delineation of the principle of self-creation that Adam has learned—and how the freedom to make mistakes is at its core, and at its creator's core.

Further, we are being stared in the face by an embryonic awareness of ecology and the interdependence of all life. Primitive religions understand such interdependence, but here it is more separated from the mythology of spirits—or at least it has become so, in the scroll our editor, Devorah, has preserved. —D.R.

ADAM:
Then two worlds here, one
the world of feelings only mine
each thing with his own
mirrored in his mate
meanwhile the plants must speak to everything
to be tended, shape their leaves to catch
the wind and shape it with their need
You need learn, they say, to understand us
beings from another world

come to inhabit
a world of feelings as within yourself
a tree will grow within you
like a mother or father, and all around
lovely trees to eat from
and lively to the mind of man
"Listen to the wind among leaves"
echoes in my bones
Each plant needs a world of others
to find its hidden mate
animals already are being taught at each bush
drinking deep of nectar
more is all they want and fly
or walk or crawl to another flower
These plants must be the priests of life
also its prophets, pointing the way
while setting a table
and busy in their workrooms making
the air we'll need to breathe
How do I listen to the air itself
except through the trees dangling
tongues of branches and leaves
while the hair of the grasses is ruffled
by restless winds: my breath—
the breathings of all the animals—
mimics the mothering trees.

CHAPTER 25

A further meditation on being alone even within the Garden is modeled upon the ancient epics as they portray the birth of language. Adam catalogs the natural world and once again deduces from it the development of knowledge and memory. We find such catalogs popular today among our poets, and Solomon's Song also drew upon this chapter. However, our poets show their modernity by clinging to the sensuality of the body in their inventories of seduction.

Unlike his earlier dreams, the true Eve is already within Adam's inward thought as he conceives of her.

By speaking to Eve in imagination, Adam confirms a place within himself that is outside the Garden's realm—that is, human consciousness. —D.R.

ADAM:
Is this body all I have?
All else I contain in mind
when I face it, yet where was I
when it filled with the fish of words?

When I saw for the first time
a world swimming in my head?
Because I recognized it: it was I
but here my creator set me
to crawl ashore in a great library
of the natural world, to read
the texts of plants, hear the arguments
of animals and the wild wind
from other worlds with this restless mind
moved to learn at a leaf
master the map of hidden roots
follow the road from nostril to flower
to discover desire
dusting me with its future
its will to seed, be everywhere
protect the future not itself
under her sheltering tree of knowledge
to look up and unearth the stars
stare them in their multitude of faces
stars the sleeping mind reads
to know our history and drink
the wine of memory
smell the spices of a mother's breast
and know it can only be she
honey and milk beneath her tongue
her lips of cream
oh sister my Eve
the tree shields prior smells
you as well are a garden enclosed
a fountain sealed, a tree within
mothering fields of frankincense

cinnamon and myrrh
who but I will blow upon my Garden
as the wind, freeing the scents
that awaken eyes in the mind:
a silent uproar of colors
I walk up and down
as in a gallery of flowers
where I have come into my world
to eat and drink with my wife, my daughter
my fountain, root, spring, well.

CHAPTER 26

Now Eve has discovered the mistaken identity of Samael, determining the mistake to be simply a misnaming. She resolves to hide the knowledge, with the help of the fruit of the tree of knowing, which the snake has extolled. Thus, as hidden knowledge has entered creatures, the need for Wisdom occurs, which Eve has already contemplated as her mother.

I believe this allegory is behind the religious cult which presumes to speak to God in secret languages, and which still emphasizes the Shekhinah's power. The implied meaning in the Book of Paradise is that if secret knowledge is to become manifest, it must leave the Garden, for it can only exist outside it.

EVE:
His secret lodges within me
how could I have felt wrong?
I will hide this knowledge
I will be another Eve
so time has begun
nectar, drink of gods, opens my eyes
I am alive—another Eve died
ambrosial smell on her
I will carry boughs of innocent fruit.

C H A P T E R   2 7

A further dream of Eve, confused with Lilith, and a
source most popular for Solomon and today's court
love poetry.

A D A M :
I hear her singing a long way off
the words are lost in the wind
yet she comes closer
I see her face, her cheeks shining
outlined by rubies
her neck gleaming gold
a pomegranate tree attended by pines
as she moves closer, revealing hips
crafted with cunning art: blinding junctions
nonpareils, thighs struck gemlike
from the artist's mind, who nestled there
between them, a wine-filled womb.

CHAPTER 28

As Adam eats the fruit, Lilith turns into a veiled Eve,
listening in the bushes. This we have seen depicted
in the Canaanitish scrolls, but the scene of Adam's
first bite must have been too much to bear for the
priests and has clearly been erased.

ADAM:
I must eat to be
a partner of Eve—to know her
as you, my snake
have grasped my will
to mistake her—
Will you climb for me also
as your male snake mounted for Eve?
[*bites*]
I was looking at a text of grass
but gently moving over it
black leaves, a lacework tree
what are these shadows but the book
of unknowing: all that is seen
must be forgotten—and returned by the sun.
This the plants know by their roots
in darkness and water. This they encode

in brilliance for our senses:
tasting with our eyes
feeling with our mouths, seeing with our hands
and a fragrant essence blown
into our nostrils
a colorless texture read by heart
and now we must seek each other
also in darkness.

CHAPTER 29

Having eaten the fruit, Eve tries to make sense of new thoughts about her world, remembering the place where their secrets were first shared, evidently a bower she constructed together with Adam. When was this? There is no trace in the scroll of her having yet met Adam, and in fact they appear to meet for the first time in a scene of congress farther on in the tale. It might appear to an uneducated listener that additional chapters have been excised, but in fact I surmise that our chapters are in proper order and that the voices of Eve and Adam in this portion of the scroll conjure dreams and memories in order to construe death. After all, they are recently under the influence of the fruit of knowing.

It falls to Eve to describe their situation as a catastrophe. Responsibility for each other has now become their refuge from despair. Prior to the mistaken identities of the snakes, no responsibilities were present in Paradise; Adam and Eve did what came naturally, naming and tending. Now intimacy will be something requiring submission, a trust that when broken will lead to the same feelings of unnaturalness and error as the congress with snakes.

Instead of boundless pride, the creatures will know mistakes and uncertainty, and from the glory of naming, they will learn fear of betrayal. Their integrity will now be based on vows they make to each other.

Is it a fall? If so, it's a fall from pride, which now has to be regained alongside the pain of feeling betrayed and the struggle of submitting to another's often unknown wishes.
—D.R.

EVE:
Time is the form of sentience
where all is knowing
even the shadows are etched
in memory—nothing forgotten, just stored
in our darkness and water. Water
and earth we carry with us, unearthed
in moments of creation
when we know ourselves as the God intended
his bride, himself: the song, the singer
the book and its mirror: his mother, her father
now we are joined in our own world
where death is the roof over us
keeping a secret
as the first house we built
our garden arbor: made to look as natural
as his creation but more fixed
like thought before it blossomed
into flowers, erected
into great trees, and told

in the diverse words we learned there
to avoid death. Our catastrophe
forces us to be responsible
for each other, submit to
intimacy sheltered from heaven
harboring good and bad within
And vow to hold to each other
as good and bad befall us.

*The Lost
Book of
Paradise*

CHAPTER 30

Eve returns to her confusion of Samael with Adam, in a description of sexual congress that is all the rage in our poetry now. Yet here it is more starkly primitive, as Eve describes congress with Samael in the frightening absence of mutual responsibility. Can we even conceive of a Paradise as flawed as this one? Our Garden of Eden must have rules of right and wrong strictly observed. Although the lovers in our songs often prove love stronger than certainty and our writers may sympathize with Adam and Eve, God's way is always right. Unfortunately, for this reason our history has been cast into prose and misses the poetry of our love songs, where uncertainty creates excitement and heaven can be ignored in its predictability.

After the fall—or the mistakes—the two human beings have ideal memories of their mates that can never be met in reality. The danger of their sexual appetite is that it breeds desire for more than is real, where in the Garden everything sufficed. The implied morality is that what we learn from the necessity of restraint is how to learn from the mistakes of others, which Adam and Eve could not do in

Eden. So the tale criticizes the gods for not giving them a past, and from this indictment may have come the more rigid morality of a unisexual God. —D.R.

E V E :
When I first reached for Adam's flesh
the reaching already held
more than I could possess
for I needed more than him, an
acceptance that bears the secret within
an embrace that hid the secret between us
so I would never need to know
how to tell it, the seed
held deep beneath my breast
unshown to even him, a pain unknown
(was it me?) biting
into myself as I tasted his mouth
as if thus he planted it there
—yes, I did swallow it
some air I breathed and shouldn't have:
it wasn't for me. Why, then, quick heart?
It was too late—all I can remember
nothing before or since, since
I wasn't there when it happened, another Eve
must be hidden in the Garden, I know
there is another Adam
to whom I would turn as my right arm
turns when I pillow my head
to star-gaze, enrobed by jewel points
he is my king and starfruit tree
I would sit down under his shadow in delight

tasting his sweet fruit
until I was sick with love, nursed
by the perfumes of his neck
on my shoulder, the lemons beneath his tongue
he is my father and son
as I am all to him
his left hand under my head
his right embraces my body
our bed is green
our house of cedar and fir.

CHAPTER 31

Following hard on the sexual congress comes Eve's description of her first encounter with Adam, in the form of a memory. This chapter reminds us again of Adam's and Eve's inward confusion, brought on by the bite into the godly realm of wisdom.

Eve has witnessed Adam naming and learns as well that he mistook the snake. The mystery in this chapter may suggest the way memory works to absorb knowledge that is too catastrophic to face. Certainly our priests will interpret it thus, just as they will forbid the scroll's being read by any but qualified scholars. There appears to be a tragic nobility to Eve's confrontation with her fate, one that Adam never achieves.

The penultimate comment here by Devorah was erased but made legible again with microscopy. Was it she herself who excised it? —D.R.

EVE:

When I came upon you I was veiled by ferns
watching you like a king at his table
animals brought you presents of fruit:

No, no, you would say, I must gather
by myself, to know the source and name it
Then, a parrot—you called it—fixed you
in its eye: Why does everyone stop what they do
when I appear? What makes your eye
widen? A beauty, you replied,
of dazzling color: I am transfixed
before this large head and chromatic crown
this beauty clears ideas away
rising like clouds high above us
dull birds from image-breeding language
Are you the female, you asked?
"Are you the female?" she shrieked
her beak clasping a lock of your hair
as she hopped onto your toes;
you ran your hands beneath her plumage
to grasp flesh, nuzzling the fuzzy green
head. You make light of me,
you continued, but it is an excitement
Are you my mate?
"My mate," she replied, and you slumped
at her short feet
"Yet I have another
with whom such speaking is all reds, yellows and blues"
Oh, you seemed to know my mind, you moaned
I have also known another, you said
when I lay with the snake
And that was the first I heard of it.

CHAPTER 32

The nobility of Eve's thoughts, as she recounts what
Adam learned earlier, is here delivered in the finest
archaic Hebrew poetry yet discovered. Although
unfamiliar with the scroll as a whole, poets today
remain under its influence from tradition, so that
again I find phrases renewed in Solomon's Song,
among others.

Beyond what Lilith and Samael have already con-
veyed, Eve has conceived that the thoughts reproduced by language are the same ones with which the
plants have reproduced food. The nectaries of flowers, which seduce the small animals [*ants*—D.R.], resemble the ambrosia of gods, so that Eve has deduced
how food is converted into knowledge.

There is no mention of water. In the Canaanitish
scrolls, water is the province of heaven and of a male
god, and his interaction with the earth is portrayed
as sexual congress. The Hebraic poet has transformed this myth into a history of human origins
that, while natural, provides a basis for the unique
Hebraic emphasis on learning. The Book of Paradise
provides a poetic myth for reading the natural world
as a scroll.

Today this myth has been transformed further into our understanding of love and responsibility between man and woman, as we hear in our new poems and histories. In the same way, the respect for trees recorded in David's psalms inspires their comparison to the most learned scholar.

It is not too presumptuous to discern in Devorah's comments an ancient understanding of the chemistry of human thought. While we do find a rudimentary precursor of evolutionary ecology, there is as yet little intuition of chemical processes and, beyond that, genetics. Perhaps chemistry, like water, would have involved the domain of the male god.

Nevertheless, the equation of fruiting plants with creative intelligence is remarkable, considering that this primitive culture could not have known that flowering plants appeared very late in evolution. The culture we are confronting here was not yet agricultural, and so we find that their image of Eden is decidedly more tropical—and oasis-like—than the later biblical version. This Hebraic people's horticulture must have established ties to the tropics, where rain and water are in such abundant quantities they may be taken for granted. —D.R.

EVE:
So Adam was also betrayed by his senses
sovereignties mirrored by snakes
now we must think, see beyond
in order to pass
what stands in memory
first, reflected love—but no

it was need and not even ours
we were meant to rehearse a leaving
learn two languages, outer
and inner shapes and sounds
so we make our own new world
start: sound is the language of ear
color and shape of all the others
light, touch, taste and smell
as all shape a memory
of my first seeing and unalterable love
for it was me and all I sense was
once untangled
singular—where now I love complexly
all things growing intricate
needing my focus: desire
does it, concentrates one
Adam, and done, all else blurs
losing the diverse Eden I learned
from angels and demons, now the flowers
and winds. Oh, bag of myrrh
between my breasts, you are him
and in his ear a vineyard in which I blow
small whitish flowers that spoke there
in Eden while I held him
Adam, your eyes were speaking parrots
from your heart, and now the knowledge
of them—birds and eyes entangled—pulls
my mind back to you, as you sat up
and we watched a column of ants
How long have they been here—to multiply so high?
you wondered, as they tended the acacia tree,
grooming it, warning

away leaf eaters, redirecting
the climbing vines, accepting the tree's offering:
sweet ant nectar
Who directs this arm of ants? you asked
What if no one, I responded
as even our longing is purposely undirected
so that we may learn—as the ants learn
from the tree—we, from memory
that branches out like the tree that taught it—
all a flexible chaos, that allows
the back and forth of remembering
a sweetness encasing what must be forgotten
first seduction, and so we want more
reproducing like night and day
and as trees bend to the changing light
even the ants follow the movement
in a dance with the tree
they multiplied, serving the sugar
in each flower, as I tasted the nectar in the boughs
of your thighs, sweet
that memory now doubles each moment
until an hour reproduces the column
of diligent ants—as my industry leaves me empty,
even more hungry for you. Unknown
to you, time is kept by the trees and grasses
and the ants we saw were taught to tend them
as we learned to tend by planting seed
to see within each the minute plant
embraced by all the food it needs
to grow, a seedling.

CHAPTER 33

Adam here compares his new knowledge of inwardness with his earlier state of mind in Paradise. He is
already aware of being beyond Paradise, as if an-
ticipating being thrown outside of the Garden. And
he realizes that commitment to one in intimacy will
be necessary and difficult, as if he knows there will
be other men and women.

Most poignantly, Adam remembers his creation
from the earth and anticipates his return to it. This
knowledge of death proceeded from his eating.

ADAM:
What is missing? I look outside and see
something remains inside—and if I look there
I miss Paradise
as though lost. Yet my mate is here
and all I see brings recognition
Isn't recognition everything?
Everything comes to me for it: live things for naming
dream things for pictures
of myself; I recognize I was there, in the ground
awaking here to grasp each thing, one after one
to embrace myself as one of two

one can be forgotten
and then, the loss distinguished
recognition takes hold by leaving
back to the first: *recognized*
back again, another acknowledgment
love is an old friend
suddenly discovered in something new, a tug
at the heart from the earth
home lost—and found in loss
as I imagine it: what if I lost this one
my lover and friend unfaced, gone
the prisoner inside I couldn't free
until I made a new home in someone's eye
who named *me*, taking
us both in
always two—one still waiting in empty Paradise
as if she were here and gone, passed
unclear what to do
Stop thinking? Can she cease
remembering I'm here, or I stop finding
myself a man, wishing to penetrate further?

CHAPTER 34

Samael and Lilith appear together and resemble
mates. But this chapter also anticipates the current
mystical theology, which absorbs the two into one,
making Samael and Lilith two aspects of the same
demon. Here they are not yet considered demons,
for only the wind embodies demons, who in the end
will be summoned in a great whirlwind.

In this ancient scroll we learn that there is no will
to disobey but rather a capriciousness to creation
itself, so that catastrophe is comparable to natural
disaster. The archaic Hebrew religion, we know,
was based upon a catastrophe of creation in heaven
itself. Even earlier, our most ancient poetry
abounded with images of volcanoes and earthquakes
as traumatic events. In our current history, a flood
assumes catastrophic proportions, and although
there is no remorse associated with it, life must assume responsibility for its disobedience of Yahweh's
will.

*The archaic religion to which Devorah refers resembles the
later development of Kabbalah—specifically, catastrophe
creation—as we know it today, although its precedents no*

doubt are archaic. The capriciousness to which Devorah refers might be considered modern today, a notion of chance or relative knowledge.

Still, there was no developed concept of evil at this time, and it was represented largely as natural catastrophe. There was, however, a revealed sense of moral responsibility for intimacy—a depiction of love and commitment quite modern in its assumption of personal accountability.

Pride was the cause of the fall: Adam broke the balance of Paradise by having felt incapable of mistakes, of doing wrong. This corresponds to modern psychology's view of the origin of anxiety toward authority, as well as the institution of incest taboo to forbid copulating "mistakes."
—D.R.

LILITH:
As we have shed our skin
the human puts one on, but
they call it, hide
a hiding skin
away from fear of error
terror the stranger
I embodied as a mirror
knowing more than gods yes to die
for not withdrawing, captive tissue
yet every sinew is craved by spirits
never to live in flesh
not know nakedness, enter no portal
for home is what the creator makes
inside his image he built unwalled pride
I could be anything for Adam.

SAMAEL:
I was everything for Eve
the God who gave them naming power
hid from them knowledge of mistakes
she could not see herself
could know no wrong she thought
not knowing her mother attendant in her fruit
everything is here, right and wrong.

*The Lost
Book of
Paradise*

CHAPTER 35

After the intoxication upon first digesting knowledge, leading to a confusion of the sequence of
events, Adam and Eve now see each other plainly for
the first time. Something more than recognition
takes place, more than the identification of themselves in each other, following the way of naming in
Paradise. In heaven also, the mode of recognition
and congress involves angelic beings who melt into
one another.

We find here the tradition of Adam calling Eve his
sister, as we have carried it over into Solomon's
Song. Although only the first couple could be both
brother and sister, lovers and friends, the noblest love
is now idealized in their image.

ADAM:
These arms to hold you
fit perfectly, as these legs
enfold—such joyous
perfection, member in the midst swelling
to enter the vestibule, dew-brushed—
a new morning breaks there, my sister
You are more than mate, my mirror

my measure of joy: beauty
a thing greater than I can recognize
not a thing recalled from the Garden
but holding all in the Garden
and the Garden in one—
in one body, one face.
More than any purpose I could imagine
beauty as beyond me
as the Garden created anew each dawn.

EVE:
My beautiful man
more than my mind can grasp—world of beauty
my eyes have been made to hold
ears to entwine, tongue to enter
nose to extract its essence
my happiness, each part of me singing
a chorus in perfect harmony—I listen
hearing your voice entire.

CHAPTER 36

The great whirlwind that blew away the Garden
seems childlike and more befitting a fairy tale, for it
makes the Garden seem a dream. The flood story in
our contemporary's history is depicted with far
clearer purpose. Yet it is probable that the missing
chapter of the Scroll of Paradise occurred here and
reported the ferocity of the Garden's storm. The
author may have traveled in Africa or India or to the
sea islands, witnessing such a storm's handiwork.

Although the demons were hidden in Eden's
winds, they must have been blown away too in this
storm, along with the angelic flowers.

Now we have a more realistic sense of our history
and can place the Garden in the past and in a real
location, while the force that ushered Adam and Eve
from it comes from a more responsible source, a God
whose angels acted on behalf of us, in a lesson about
the nature of right and wrong. Although the whirlwind might have magnified the force of all the demons in the winds, the reason for the punishment is
not stated, implying that gods themselves were capable of mistakes and that humans must pay unnatu-
rally for the mistake of Eden. In other words, we

cannot imagine what evil can create a catastrophic storm.

The Hebrews of this time still lived close to nature and imagined the human appetite as unnatural, with its secret lives and ways of learning. Now we know it is our human superiority to the rest of creation that allows us to rise above our bodies and natural processes. In the tale of the great flood, there is a moral purpose to the catastrophe, a cleansing. It would be unusual for a writer to suggest there could have been any mistake associated with catastrophe.

And what does the destruction of Paradise accomplish? The Scroll of Paradise does not rise to a certainty of vision. In this archaic Hebrew age, there appears no decisive attempt to grasp the past, so that a destructive storm, of the kind sailors talk about at the ends of the earth, bears no lessons. This attitude befits a culture of wanderers recently settled, and it is important to preserve it, for it contains our roots.

In our time, this history of quaint tales and magnificent poems that include the Scroll of Paradise allows us more sympathy for court writers today, as they tend the tradition by the hand of wit and wisdom, transforming and renewing.

The Book of Paradise more resembles a love tale, like the Song of Solomon, than a tale of origins, primarily because it focuses so closely upon the relationship of Adam and Eve. However, the book contains vestiges of tales about the souls in heaven, which we see resurfacing later in Jewish tradition. These become full blown in the medieval Kabbalah,

*which details the midnight intercourse of God and the
Shekhinah. It is in the* Zohar *of the great poet Moses de
León, in particular, where the reunion of male and female
Jewish gods echoes its great beginnings—lost to us, as
Devorah Bat-David implies, by agency of the prudish edit-
ing of priests.*

*A further stylistic note must be made of the prehistory
of the choral convention. Apparently unknown to the author of the Book of Paradise, nevertheless a sophisticated
forerunner of the chorus is found in the diaphonic ordering
of chapters. There may have been Canaanite precedents for
this, but unfortunately Devorah omits this type of observa-
tion.* —D.R.

EVE:
Now as we lay in our hut
the winds roused, the demons stirred
began to howl
the creator sent a great whirlwind
we clung to the ground
all was lifted away, the Garden lifted
our faces clung to dirt, our hands to rocks
our home was gone and we lived
it was quieter than before
the creatures had scattered, the birds flown
flowers had sent their seed beyond seeing
we wandered, wandered
here and there we scratched roots to eat
until we came to a forest
then I heard in a dream
the Shekhinah's voice: Here,

I am where I am
she had entered the world
supplanted the tree we ate from
all we had known became hidden
but we closed our eyes and found her
mother of wisdom
to provide all we know
as the plants had taught us in the Garden
we would tend for our lives
fill up the land with others and our thoughts
where angelic nature had been
struggling to listen with mistaking ears
to plants of the field and forest
through a forest of noise
sow cities, reap the sweat
of our brow and lie down
producing the fruit of a mother's womb
each Adam each Eve a maker of space
room for the Garden in memory: the work
of naming shared again, become
a fight to speak straight.

ADAM:
Now all must be learned by mistake
listen to the birds to fly
on song to the Garden
a memorized moment and climb
back again, remembering
the price for our bodies is death
all the angels and demons would gladly pay
souls plentiful in heaven

here we build a house
to share our mistakes in secret
to share our bodies free from mistaking
an intimate shelter free from the light
to not tell giving from getting—the same
confusion as was in the Garden, here we name love
love is stronger than death
returning to the angels
we are lost in each other, disembodied
the flowers speak to us
even the snakes who taught us
seduction by thought, protection
against error: we see clearly in the mirror
ourselves, reproduced, models
we create again as seductive words
milk of intelligence
learnt at the breast of trees.

CHAPTER 37

The demons, if they were indeed employed, must have delighted in the great whirlwind as they could not among the gentle breezes of Eden.

This comment by Devorah seems out of place at this chapter and perhaps belongs to the chapter edited out. Devorah herself implies there was an "editing out" of the gods, possibly due to the female God. If so, a grand poetic justice is rewarded the original poet, whose own God attempted no less, albeit indirectly.

Devorah may have wished to allude to a tradition behind the Book of Paradise itself, a more typically Canaanite heroic epic involving the gods as characters. Thereby, the new genre this book exemplifies is one in which the human characters have acquired god attributes by virtue of their own self-reliance. As we see in this chapter, they are a couple and equal, prefiguring the Song of Solomon's lovers. That is to say, they are gods projected into the ancient human modernity of social classes and monarchy—and transcending that circumstance by human love. The older epics presented them in godlike fantasy, fulfilling the fertility rites of the earth. —D.R.

ADAM:
Love has no end
no beginning, just as it was
in the Garden
there we began in the name of love
motherless
who is origin now of all we know
the one thing we recognize
leaving home: a stranger's arms
are hers when they are ours.

EVE:
Your arms, my love, best
memory of Paradise, my hunger
to mother filled there,
my brother, flesh of mine recalled
tasted, my groom, thirsted for
my dove in his pool, my friend
breast to breast.

CHAPTER 38

The whirlwind has blown the Garden away. What the scroll wants us to learn, it seems, is that only a Garden where the wisdom of the Shekhinah does not need to be hidden could be Paradise. Now, beyond the Garden, she would rule, hidden but accessible to Adam and Eve's thought, and to all creatures as well, as food.

It appears Adam and Eve woke to find their shelter gone and all the Garden as they knew it scattered to the ends of the earth. Perhaps God put them to sleep during the whirlwind, for the experience Eve relates of it is minor. But now Adam and Eve focus on a mutual need they have recognized, for intimacy to shelter their inwardness as a roof covers their heads.

ADAM:
We have woken to create ourselves outside
we are unnatural now
in boundless appetites
safe only in secret
intimacy returning us
to our bower in the Garden, imagining

all without, all that's unseen, as Paradise
unnatural as gods whose words
make anything live
or die, in mistakes our hopes
bewildering diversity, imagining
ourselves far from our trees
while carrying them wordless with us
seduced by these tacit parent gods
vanished with all that was scattered
to be seen would ask to be misnamed
leaving us their breath and vision
of time to fall into, relenting death.

CHAPTER 39

Until they have reason for secrets, Adam and Eve in the Garden are like children, just as they appear in our contemporary's history of Yahweh's people, Israel. Then they are transformed into ideal parents, creating a home, and for the first time in ancient scrolls their marriage supplants the marriages of the gods, such as are observed by the majority of people today. Here we recognize the process that has led to the understanding in our time of one God in his male and female aspects.

Eve's final words achieve an ennobling acceptance of the tempest that has devastated Eden. By linking the loss of Paradise with the acquisition of wisdom, she recalls the heavenly commandment to tend the Garden that God imparts to Adam in our current history of creation. As Eve intimates that Paradise remains in memory as a childhood, the influence upon our religion today and its conception of the children of God are obvious.

EVE:
Our secrets formed an intimacy
denying the world's own covering

Wisdom, fearless of death
exposure is unknown to her
she is within not somewhere without
all is inside the Garden
now we have climbed outside
to find all hidden
like the gods—our wisdom in allowing Paradise
to exist in memory beyond
any blowing wind
life is not a beginning and death not an end
neither can we remember our bearing earth
or hold on
to it, like grass the moist night
or leaves their limbs in a tempest
all flesh is grass.

Background and

Commentary

1.

i. The Nature of Disease

A generation ago, Earth had not yet been revealed as a sensitive environment. Instead, the fear for survival of the human species was centered in man himself. It was the evil inclination in men that threatened nuclear war, which would be launched by a hand insensitive to human life. This notion of evil could be found in the anchoring text of Western culture, the Bible, and its genesis in the Garden of Eden story.

What has happened to that primal text, now that we find evil can be rooted in an insensitivity to *non*human life? A provocative reinterpretation of biblical metaphors has ensued, ranging among popular studies as different from one another as Carl Sagan's *The Dragons of Eden,* Elaine Pagels's *Adam, Eve, and the Serpent,* and *The Book of J,* co-authored by Harold Bloom and myself. A common thread throughout is that evil is not an animus toward other human beings but rather an insensitivity in men and women toward their mother earth.

In our age of reinterpretation, we've grown more sensitive to the biases we hold against civilizations of the past, and these range from Native American cultures to the biblical culture that produced the Garden of Eden story. Who wrote the Garden of Eden story? The Book of Genesis relates two stories that are roughly interwoven, and the older and more powerful of these was written by an author designated J by scholars. If we can now discard our biases, religious and otherwise, we find a skilled and worldly poet, most probably a court writer among the many employed by the Solomonic monarchy. The crucial knowledge is that J's retelling of the story, which existed in many earlier versions, takes for granted that we share certain assumptions about evil. Yet these notions were bypassed by subsequent Judaic and Christian religious cultures.

The most accurate translation for the tree of knowledge in Genesis is "the tree of knowing good and bad." Since the snake in the story is no more nor less supernatural than any other creature in the Garden, where can we look to understand the question that has plagued interpreters for millennia: Why didn't Adam and Eve—or even the snake—die after eating dangerous fruit? All sorts of ingenious answers have been provided, but few readers have looked at the text through the eyes of the ancient reader.

In those days, knowledge of horticulture and agriculture dominated the sciences in Hebrew culture, and the history of nomadic Hebrews was already ancient history—as well as a mocking myth employed by the older and more sophisticated Philistine culture, which has now been identified as Mycenaean Greek. (The Philistines—or Greek Sea People—were in turn satirized by some biblical writers and demeaned by others.) A great debate raged over the nature of disease, and death was thought to come by way of disease to humans as it did to plants.

Then as now, disease was understood in the broadest sense of the word: a standard medical textbook today defines it as "the pattern of response of a living organism to some form of injury . . . ranging from infection with a virus to stress from crowding to depression from loss"—to disorder in function as well as alteration in structure. If Adam and Eve were exposed to disease after eating dangerous fruit, there was no need for them or anything else alive to die instantly. And so, life as we know it outside the Garden of Eden began as a struggle against disease; trees and creatures today are the product of millions of years of strategies against disease—or death, as J might have understood it.

Before the biblical Book of Genesis, however, lie several hundred years of written Hebraic texts that are now lost, though several are referred to by name in the Bible. The Scroll of Paradise was probably the source familiar to the earliest biblical writers; although written fifty years before the establishment of the monarchy, it was the product of a Hebraic culture that was settling the land and cultivating fruits and plants. Not only was death understood as disease then, but the Scroll of Paradise described a vision of Eden that would explain how death was a product of heaven, transferred into the world by its creator.

A similar view applies to the Bible's Song of Solomon. The lovers are Adam- and Eve-like, equal and unashamed, and not only does death as a punishment seem unknown to them but a crucial line satirizes it: "for love is stronger than death." Again, this is not a punishing death but the diseaselike image of death in Solomon's time, making his authorship more likely, for the poet suggests that love is a strategy strong enough to combat any disease.

ii. The Nature of Isolation

Is the Garden of Eden story a tragedy? In the Scroll of Paradise (*Sefer Gan Eden*) and remarkably preserved as well in Genesis, the classic requirements for tragedy are met, including the mistaken identities that prevail in Greek myth.

What was the frailty in noble Adam and Eve that brought

about their fall? Although not perfect, as tragic characters cannot be, they were seduced into thinking so. How could they have
thought otherwise? They awoke in a perfect Paradise. Beauty
and luscious food did not seduce them, but as chief gardeners
(God created them to *tend* the garden, as Genesis confirms) they
learned the art of seduction itself from trees.

As early Hebraic culture would observe in its groves of fruit
trees, plants seduce animals to serve them, enticing them first
with flowers and the rewards of heavenly nectar, later with fruit,
nut, and seed. Adam and Eve were seduced by two paternal
trees, the first of which—the tree of knowing—they could not
ignore, even as they were created to know an anxiety in eating
from it.

How did this happen? First, they mistook the identity of the
snake. That mistake yielded a need to see themselves, to know
who their true mates were, for unlike the other living creatures,
Adam and Eve were created alone. Adam learned loneliness
from naming the animals; his frailty lay in assuming that Eve
was already created, out of pride in his senses, which he trusted
to find her.

Eve, created later while Adam slept, likewise presumed she
would know Adam as surely as herself, and this presumption
prompted the male snake, Samael (in later times known as
Satan). Although the snake kept his identity a secret from Eve,
Adam also hid a secret from her: his earlier encounter with
Lilith, the female snake. Adam and Eve finally knew each other
by their secrets, a loneliness turned into intimacy, a shared
secrecy. Unlike all other creatures, they were created with an
anxiety—or repressed knowledge—that something was missing.
It was as if their lack of memory could not protect them from
needing to know themselves.

This was a knowledge entitled to gods. But look what happened by the time Genesis was being written: the female component of God was repressed by the creation of Adam, who was created in the image of the one God and therefore perfect in himself, mateless. Now, it's the role of the gods in tragedy to prepare the fateful conditions. We pity the humans whose error becomes ours, since we are also innocent of the ways of gods. As humans we must long to seduce a mate—and in that longing we're innocent of the memory of parents, blind to our erotic prehistories.

The tragedy of Adam and Eve was their *need* to know themselves, to become their own parents. In sympathizing with the need, we feel the horror of the final seduction. The two trees, knowledge and life—no doubt male and female—were shrouded in taboos of incest and patricide: do not touch, do not eat. Whose trees were these? The gods'. The climactic scene of admiring, touching, and eating is as fateful as Oedipus discovering that his wife and his mother are the same person.

I have already enlarged upon Genesis, but it's not hard to tell that the J version of Genesis is incomplete and the edited, or redacted, version of Genesis is inconsistent. In the original Hebraic version of the Eden story, the Scroll of Paradise, both Adam and Eve confronted their snakes alone. We can surmise this from the commentary on the scroll that has survived, after the composition of the Scroll of Paradise in about 1075 B.C.E. This preceded the oldest part of Genesis by a hundred and fifty years, and it remained extant through several hundred years, referred to in Hebraic Midrash and Agadah as the Scroll of Paradise (*Sefer Gan Eden,*) alongside a story that extended beyond Eden, the Scroll of the History of Adam. This commentary extends all the way into the Middle Ages, through the

Talmud and the Kabbalah—though even by 500 B.C.E. the sages were quoting memory and not the existing scrolls.

This much we know from the Bible as we have it today: Adam was given the task of naming the flora and fauna of the Garden, and he was motivated by the desire to discover his mate. Whatever God intended by creating Adam alone, Adam assumed his mate existed, just like the mates of all other species. So the Book of Paradise, from which Genesis drew its model, is a story of search, a quest that ends in loss.

A desire to know and feel each living thing is given to Adam: all animals, even insects, were human size in the Garden, walked upright, and spoke. Like other animals, Adam and Eve could not see themselves but they had a higher capacity for language: metaphor, the associative naming power, a reproduction of images. However, the plants alone were of great variety in size, some trees awe-inspiring in height, and it was they who taught Adam and Eve to speak the language of reproduction that they alone possessed. For the plants needed to reproduce—and needed Adam's tending—in order to furnish the food for all other creatures.

The drama of Adam and Eve develops in the context of tending the plants and naming; words give more life to each living thing. Their own private worlds could be conceived by them, internalized and kept secret, obliging imaginative language as communication—in the name of love. And I believe it was in the name of love that the Book of Paradise portrayed both humans eating from the forbidden tree, for Adam and Eve had nothing to lose from opening their eyes to an isolation they already experienced. We might say that love saved them—but also blinded them. Even death was known by them in the Garden, as they watched fallen leaves fertilize the earth.

Rediscovered by a scholar at Solomon's palace library, the Book of Paradise might have aroused enthusiasm in memory of the dead king's love of vineyards and gardens. King Solomon in his day was famous for his royal gardens, his importation of tropical species. The Garden of Eden is tropical, the fruits and herbs there encompassing a wider variety than popularly known. The poet's imagination might range further, yet the understanding that plants precede humans—and that animal life is dependent on them—is clear from the commentary on this lost book.

The many volumes of surviving Hebraic commentary on the Bible's Song of Solomon refer to the lovers in that Edenic scroll as Adam and Eve, though they are unnamed in the Bible itself. It is inescapable that the Song of Solomon was modeled upon the Book of Paradise. In no ancient book other than Song of Solomon is a woman's voice and consciousness presented at greater length than a male's, although J's Genesis appears to have been written by a woman. And in no surviving biblical book is the natural world so lovingly addressed, not only suggesting Solomonic authorship but also a lost tradition of edenic scrolls and poetry.

What holds true in Genesis is that Adam's purpose in the Garden is to be its gardener; he was put there expressly to tend it. Plants were created first and by themselves provided the conditions for animal life. Later, plants seduced animals with their talent for beauty, mimicry, and reproductive strategy, persuading them with flowers and nectar to help pollinate and otherwise reproduce their fruits and, later, to eat them and disperse their seeds. The archaic Hebrew poet who composed the Scroll of Paradise would have learned much about plants from the cultivation of orchards and vineyards that burgeoned among the settled tribes of Israel. Plants possessed natural secrets that humans beheld with awe; nature was not to be simply dominated but lived beside and *tended*—the active verb surviving in Genesis. At this time all local cultures, the Hebrews included, cultivated sacred groves.

The Hebraic tradition lost touch with its early epic scrolls when survival became an unfortunate but necessary preoccupation, beginning in the eighth century B.C.E. Gone was the memory of gardens and the epics that embraced nature, though the Song of Solomon remained as a substantial trace. We can see in Solomon's smaller epic not only the equality of sexes but the symbiotic relation of man's restless memory and nature's preoccupation with the present.

After the fall, loneliness in the Garden projects into the condition of isolation in the world. From human exploration of the world, biblical poets knew that different climates and different geographies—cedars of Lebanon symbolize the former in Song of Solomon and spices of the Orient symbolize the latter—these differences produced different species. We know a little more about this today thanks to Darwin and Freud, but it is all commentary; the fundamental cause known to the poet of the Book of Paradise, isolation, we now assume was brought about by the breaking up of continents and the movement of glaciers. Isolation allows for the divergence and creativity of plant species, and the species themselves colonize the land by seed dispersal: in botanic terms, the plants create diasporas of their species.

In their isolation, as plants manipulate animals to disperse their seeds, largely by offering food, the human mirror to this seduction process is human culture and the consequent explor-

ing, colonizing, and breaking away of cultures. Like Adam and
Eve's loneliness—a mutual sense that something was hidden or
missing—human cultures solve the problems of their isolation
by masks or images (mistaken identities) and then come to
knowledge of themselves as ambivalent beings, knowing both
good and evil.

iii. The Nature of Play

The greatest love epic in any Western language is the Bible's
Song of Solomon. Thousands of books were written about it over
the millennia, and many imitations persisted down through the
Middle Ages. For all the various interpretations, none has attempted to place the great poem in its own tradition.

The Song of Solomon has been compared to precursors in
older cultures, such as Egyptian love songs and Tamil love
poetry. Although no manuscripts of archaic Hebraic scrolls sur-
vive, is there any excuse for the continued observance of taboos
against imagination by secular scholars?

These taboos are enforced unawares, as the field of biblical
scholarship is saddled with the most conventional thinking in
any area of the humanities. What we'd expect to be modern, a
structuralist approach, turns out to be reactionary by replacing
the myth of a supernatural author with theories of a homogen-
ized biblical tradition. The Bible is described as a "world of
biblical literature" whose authors—writing up to nine centuries
apart—used the same linguistic idiom and shared the same
religious sentiments. Nowhere in history is there evidence for
such a static culture, except among dead cultures. By comparison, sagas in Old English have little in common with the latest
novels, and even a novelist in English from the nineteenth
century would find it hard to recognize kinship with the current

idiom. Yet we have not produced masterpieces in any greater measure than Hebraic culture in the tenth century B.C.E., and powerful Hebraic writers contributed wonderfully varied classics over many centuries.

As indication of their predisposition, biblical scholars take for granted that the Hebraic writers were parochial even when evidence suggests that writers of the time traveled, knew several languages, translated among many scripts that stretched from pictogram and cuneiform to archaic alphabets, and made use of ancient libraries throughout the known world.

A fine scholar asks, "For whom was this book written?" But in the biblical field the question is too quickly reduced to "What religious use was it put to?"—*Sitz im Leben,* the old German critics called it. Yet history has shown that the books were often written long before—decades and centuries before—they were appropriated by religion. How to avoid this fact? Modern scholars have concentrated on the redactor: that is, the religious scribe who in many ways resembles the scholars themselves in his distance from creativity. By repressing the original writers and the question of authorship, biblical academics in our day pay lip service to hoary religious taboos.

Who wrote the Book of Paradise? The clues are in the two works of the Bible most directly influenced by it, the Garden of Eden story and the Song of Solomon. Both were composed in the era just before and following Solomon's death, while the grand court of princes and princesses, poets and historians assembled to celebrate the enduring monarchy was still in high renaissance. The author of the Garden of Eden story is most reliably placed at the court of Rehoboam, Solomon's son. As I concluded in the notes to *The Book of J,* concurrent with the critic Harold Bloom's commentary, J was most likely a woman and a Solomonic princess. The author of Song of Solomon is more difficult to determine; I used to think that Solomon himself wrote it. After additional research, I've found that the most likely author was J herself.

The Book of Paradise was probably written a hundred and fifty years earlier, just before the inauguration of the Israelite monarchy, by a poet at one of the Jewish Canaanite literary centers, a writer fluent in Phoenician, Egyptian, and Mycenaean Greek who had access to the Philistine and Phoenician libraries in the coastal cities. Later, during Solomon's reign, this early Hebraic literature was collected and edited at the palace libraries, yet I trust Devorah Bat-David when she suggests that the scroll had been suppressed by priests. Devorah retranslated it from the Phoenician translation she found in a Philistine library.

Nevertheless, King David had inherited his own library of scrolls dating back through Saul and the era of Judges, consisting of history, myths, and poetry of all the various tribes. In David's palace libraries, these scrolls and aged clay tablets, many written in the early cuneiform script, were translated into the Phoenician characters that underlay early Hebrew, first by Saul's and then by David's court poets. We may assume the translations were quite freely rendered, and that the Jerusalem poets' linguistic knowledge was heightened by visits to the older, richer holdings in Egyptian, Phoenician, and Philistine Greek libraries. Those cultures had supported written documents for many centuries, and the Jerusalem poets were quite free to play with traditions to which their allegiance was literary.

Play is a critical concept to paradise myths. Paradise is a dream of meaningful play, and play entails forgetting who one is—or never knowing. For Adam and Eve in the Scroll of

Background and Commentary

Paradise, a freedom from time, gender, and self would engender their tragedy. Paradise scrolls were common to all ancient writing cultures, although at this time only the Hebraic culture was actively rewriting them, as far as we know.

2.

In the Book of Paradise, Adam plays the role of a hero on a quest to find his mate. On his journey Adam must inevitably find out what God had intended to remain hidden, and it is Eve who must show the way by conceiving of her mother. Traces of the mother, of the female aspect of God—called the *Shekhinah* in Jewish mystical tradition—have been removed or repressed in the Book of Genesis and the Song of Solomon. Yet she has remained vital in Jewish texts, most notably in the *Zohar,* written by Moses de León in a deliberate crypto-Aramaic, so as to seem far more ancient.

In the *Zohar* the Shekhinah is God's consort or bride, although this knowledge is hidden in complex allusion. Composed more than twenty centuries earlier, the Book of Paradise reveals a hidden mate of God, who has nonetheless found her place in the Garden of Eden, in the form of the tree of knowledge. The Shekhinah here embodies wisdom, as she does in later tradition, but in the Book of Paradise we are closer to her genesis, as Devorah speculates in her commentary. We are assured that even a monotheistic God must have his partner, just as Adam—created in God's image—could not be left alone without an Eve.

The character of the snake as we find it in Genesis has

been left enigmatic, but certainly there were two snakes, male and female, just as for all other living things. The two snakes have a long history in Jewish texts, particularly the Kabbalah, where they continue to be known as Samael and Lilith. In early Hebraic commentary they absorb many diverse myths and superstitions, but later in the *Zohar* the two revert to serpenthood, often changing into one another. Like the emasculated snake in Genesis, Samael and Lilith in the Book of Paradise are natural creatures, albeit the walking and talking type of subtle creature that inhabited the Garden of Eden.

The catastrophe of the whirlwind at the end of the Book of Paradise is paralleled in many biblical books, notably Job and the flood story of Genesis, where it is attributable once again to the author J. I have appended portions of the flood story from Genesis, as well as J's Garden of Eden text, at the end of this book. There I have also included a portion of the Song of Solomon for comparison with the Book of Paradise; all the new biblical translations were made from the original Hebrew by myself.

The whirlwind brings death-dealing injury to the Garden, just as the flood does to the earth, yet out of both our world emerges in greater depth—and with a stronger ability to combat disease. That ability, naturally enough in both stories, reflects a new wisdom. In the Book of Paradise in particular, Wisdom shows the way, waiting for her children like a mother if they will attend her, hidden beneath the surface of all things.

There are considerable changes and editing in the Scroll of Paradise as Devorah found it in the ninth century B.C.E. These changes were probably made under priestly supervision when the scribes copied the scroll from the old cuneiform into the Old Phoenician script, long before it was translated into Phoenician itself and then found and retranslated into Hebrew by Devorah.

Imagining the Text

Where did the Bible's story of Paradise come from? In J's biblical version derived from the creation stories of earlier times, the differences are more striking than the similarities.

The fundamental difference is literary depth—the *written* quality of the work. This is where conventional Bible scholars turn their backs on the author, unable to engage the arts beyond filibusters of theory. And it is here I began to investigate the Hebraic poetic tradition that preceded the Bible. Many early books alluded to in the Bible, however, were lost between the eighth and sixth centuries B.C.E., starting with the destruction of the palaces and archives in northern Israel and parts of Judah.

The taboos and clichés of Western culture erase this past. "Their most enduring legacy was their religion" (Margaret Oliphant, *The Atlas of the Ancient World,* 1992), is how commentators typically describe the ancient Hebrews. But no, I would argue for a Hebraic culture that produced the hundreds of writers who wrote the great poems and narratives of the Bible in the ages before religion dominated.

One day, during my research in Jerusalem, I met Professor Moshe Idel for lunch at the Hebrew University on Mount Scopus. We speculated about prebiblical Jewish religion—a subject in which Idel's insights are notable—and about the independence of the early biblical historians and poets from religion. I asked Moshe to accompany me to the new Mormon campus down the road, where tabletop models of the city of Jerusalem had been installed. Four models showed Jerusalem at different periods, and the one that drew me was the oldest: a representation of the City of David, the palaces with their archives and libraries standing but the Temple not yet conceived.

The model, however, was disappointing, although we couldn't say exactly why. But one week later I found another model of Davidic Jerusalem that was being prepared for the David's Tower Museum. Where the Mormon model appeared empty and colorless, this one teemed with life, showing tiny figures and animals in the streets, including men sitting in the coffeehouses that lined the famous street to the palace library. Shops of all kinds displayed their wares, including papyrus scrolls and writing implements.

I felt closer to home—to the reality of heritage as a home— when I found that street; it brought me closer to imagining myself alive at that time. And I could see what was within the nation's new library (its archives as well as its texts and translations from other cultures, in clay, stone, papyrus, even skins) because I had previously envisioned the early authors themselves, in my translations of *The Book of J* and *A Poet's Bible*, where I had first detected as well the caravan trade in texts among far-flung civilizations.

The tiny figures sitting in the cafés outside the palace came alive: among them would be many of the hundreds of court writers and archivists, arguing the latest translations and interpretations. I imagined one poet, having just returned from a visit to other libraries in Egypt or the Near East, recounting his or her finds there. Evidence of travel had abounded in the model: monkeys, parrots, heaps of spices; even the "tea" they were drinking suggesting Africa, India, even farther. Caravans passed through Jerusalem regularly—how can we imagine a great writer not joining one to visit foreign libraries, some just a few days' journey away?

At the same spot in Jerusalem today, on a clear afternoon, one may glimpse Tel Aviv on the coast; scholars have shunned the thought, but how unlikely it is that a writer would sit out his or her entire life in a small town like Jerusalem. When I sat in her office at the Israel Museum, discussing this with Professor Michal Dayagi, the chief Israeli curator of this period, she said, "Oh, but there were bandits on the roads and travel was dangerous." Well, would a little danger not add adventure to a poet's life, then as now?

A poet's training would also have required the translation of cuneiform texts into the new Hebrew alphabet. Poetic texts in Canaanite languages, set in clay or penned on papyrus, were already quite ancient. Even older, the classic poetic texts of Egypt and Mesopotamia would need retranslation. Can we imagine that Solomon himself did not try his hand at translating the Egyptian love poetry or Tamil love epics from India that bear such resemblance to his own Song of Solomon? (Professor Chaim Rabin, the world's leading expert on Indian influences in Ancient Hebrew, winked in approval as I suggested it over dinner one night.)

Even earlier, the major Near Eastern empire was translating archaic texts into cuneiform Hittite by the fifteenth century B.C.E. And by the time of Solomon's empire in the tenth century B.C.E., Phoenicians had translated the literary texts of Mycenaean Greece into their alphabet, a sister language to Hebrew. Hebraic poets may have worked from these translations in the Phoenician libraries, or they may have already made their own

Imagining the Text

translations into archaic cuneiform Hebrew. A Jerusalem poet need only travel to the coast to have access to Mycenaean Greek texts in an ancient palace library: recent scholarship has confirmed this spectacularly, showing that the Philistines, or "Sea People," were most likely colonizing Greeks.

The Lost Book of Paradise is an imaginary work of scholarship. As in *The Book of J,* which I previously translated, I imagined an author whom tradition has expunged. J's great text became part of Genesis, Exodus, and other books of the Hebrew Bible, so I was able to reconstruct her actual words. The words of the Book of Paradise, conversely, were entirely lost, although traces remain in the Song of Solomon and Genesis. We turn, then, to the ancient commentaries that supply details about the text. First, we must set aside the conventional scholars who provide euphemisms to conceal the Hebrew Bible's great writers. Scribes, redactors, prophets, and priests may be deferred to, but we never meet up with a professional Hebrew poet in academic studies, as is commonplace in Ancient Greek scholarship.

However, the tradition of biblical commentary called Midrash is alive with the creative daring that we miss in Bible studies and literary criticism today. The old sages knew we must experience the context of a work, its flesh and blood. Ancient scholars were not afraid to be poets. The modern scholars of the Song of Solomon prefer to call it the Song of Songs, since they don't wish to consider that Solomon would have been trained at court as a poet and translator. And few critics consult the *Midrash Shir ha-Shirim*; the depth of imagination in the ancient commentary devoted to The Song (as the rabbis called it) is foreign to scholarship in our day.

When scholars are blinded by intellectual pieties, it's time to turn to the poets, whose orientation to culture is critical and not sanctimonious. For in the great culture of ancient Israel, it was the poets who served as analysts of myths—in tandem with the biologists, botanists, and scholars of their day, tenders of the fields and palace archives.

SELECTIONS FROM

Genesis

(Selections from *Genesis*, the *Book of J* version,
translated by David Rosenberg)

1

Before a plant of the field was in earth, before a grain
of the field sprouted—Yahweh had not spilled rain
on the earth, nor was there man to work the land—
yet from the day Yahweh made earth and sky, a mist
from within would rise to moisten the surface. Yahweh shaped an earthling from clay of this earth, blew
into its nostrils the wind of life. Now look: man
becomes a creature of flesh.

2

Now Yahweh planted a garden in Eden, eastward,
settled there the man he formed. From the land Yahweh grew all trees lovely to look upon, good to eat
from; the tree of life was there in the garden, and the
tree of knowing good and bad.

3

. . . Yahweh lifts the man, brings him to rest in the
garden of Eden, to tend it and watch. "From all trees
in the garden you are free to eat"—so Yahweh
desires the man know—"but the tree of knowing
good and bad you will not touch. Eat from it," said
Yahweh, "and on that day death touches you."

4

"It is no good the man be alone," said Yahweh. "I will make a partner to stand beside him." So Yahweh shaped out of the soil all the creatures of the field and birds of the air, bringing them to the man to see how he would call them. Whatever the man called became the living creature's name. Soon all wild animals had names the man gave them, all birds of the air and creatures of the field, but the man did not find his partner among them. Now Yahweh put the man into a deep sleep; when he fell asleep, he took a rib, closed the flesh of his side again. Starting with the part taken out of the man, Yahweh shaped the rib into woman, returned her to the side of the man.

"This one is bone of my bone, flesh of my flesh," said the man. "Woman I call her, out of man she was parted." So a man parts from his mother and father, clings to his wife: they were one flesh.

And look: they are naked, man and woman, untouched by shame, not knowing it.

5

Now the snake was smoother-tongued than any wild creature that Yahweh made. "Did the God really mean," he said to the woman, "you can't eat from any tree of the garden?"

"But the fruit of the trees we may," said the woman to the snake. "Just the tree in the middle of the garden, the God said. You can't eat from it, you can't touch—without death touching you." "Death will not touch you," said the snake to the woman. "The God knows on the day you eat from it your eyes will fall open like gods, knowing good and bad."

Now the woman sees how good the tree looks, to eat from, how lovely to the eyes, lively to the mind. To its fruit she reached; ate, gave to her man, there with her, and he ate.

And the eyes of both fall open, grasp knowledge of their naked skin. They wound together fig leaves, made coverings for themselves.

9
The man named his wife Hava: she would have all who live, smooth the way, mother. . . .

[*But following, Hava would name the children: she always improves on Adam.*]

10
"Look," said Yahweh, "the earthling sees like one of us, knowing good and bad. And now he may blindly reach out his hand, grasp the tree of life as well, eat, and live forever."

Now Yahweh took him out of the Garden of Eden, to toil—in the soil from which he was taken.

The earthling was driven forward. . . .

[It is always Adam to whom Yahweh relates.]

11
Now the man knew Hava, his wife, in the flesh. . . .

18
Now look: from the earthling's first step man has spread over the face of the earth. He has fathered many daughters. The sons of heaven came down to look at the daughters of men, alive to their loveliness, knowing any they pleased for wives.

20
Now the race of giants: they were in the land then, from the time the sons of heaven entered the rooms of the daughters of men. Hero figures were born to them, men and women of mythic fame.

22
. . . "In another seven days rain spills on the land unceasing: forty days, forty nights. I will erase all that rose into living substance, spreading over the face of the earth—all which I made. . . ."

23
Now look: the seven days and the flood water is on the land. Look: the rain would be on the land, forty days, forty nights.

Yahweh shut him [*Noah*] in at the door.

24

So it was: forty days on the land, the flood; the water rose, the ark lifted up above the land.

The water overcame everything, overran the land; the ark made its way over a face of water.

Now the water was swelling fast, the earth was subdued: all the high mountains under the sky were covered.

Fifteen cubits higher grew the water, above the submerged mountains.

All living spirit on dry land—the wind of life in its nostrils—died. Erased: all that arose from the earth, earthlings from man to beast, creatures that crawl and creatures that fly. They ceased to exist, all but Noah, left alone in the ark with all his company.

APPENDIX B

SELECTIONS FROM

Song of Solomon

(Chapter Five, *Song of Solomon*,
translated by David Rosenberg)

I will be in my garden
as I am deep within you
my bride

as if you are my sister
I am rich in spices—
as if my bride, I pluck fresh myrrh

I am rich with honey
and I will eat the honeycomb whole
as well

I will have my wine, my bride
and it is pure, my sister
as milk and honey

friend, you will eat
you will drink deeply, lover
you will be rich with love, my dearest friend

I was asleep
but the soul within me
stayed awake

like my heart—true to a timeless rhythm
to which I still respond—
listen, a gentle knocking

like my heart's beating—
*Open to me, my love
my purest image, sister, dove*

*all I can imagine—my head is drenched
with dew, all my memories
melt into you*

*I would walk through nights of blinding rain
all doors locked to my presence
I would be happy in blackest exile*

*knowing you alone would not reject me
never forget
not turn away—*

. . .

But I've undone the robe of devotion
where I wrapped my naked heart before you—
how can I rise to your presence?

I've washed the feet that were tired and dirty
when I walked in the reality of your presence—
how can I stand and face myself?

. . .

My love who came inside me
whom I held firmly
whose hand was on the lock of my being

removed his arms
pulled his hand away—
I awoke and

I was drawn to him
a softness spread in me
I was open within

and then I was desolate and empty
he had gone
my heart leapt from my breast

I ran to the door
my soul overwhelmed me
my hands were drenched, as if with perfume

it was my love for him—
the lock was wet with the myrrh
of my devotion

I opened for my love
I alone was open to him
but he had gone

the one for whom I trembled
heard it from my lips
how I had turned from him when

I thought I was alone—
suddenly my soul no longer knew me
just as I had forgotten him

I was riveted with anxiety
I was as lifeless as an empty robe
I couldn't move

my feet were a statue's feet
I was lifeless clay
I was naked earth

then I wandered through the streets
looking for signs of his nearness
seeing nothing

I called, I cried
desperate for his closeness
hearing only silence

only my enemies heard me, like watchmen
patrolling my city's walls
who found me in night gown

who saw me vulnerable and alone
who struck me down
I was wounded for my distraction

my robe my dignity stripped away
I could not even pray
my heart was in my mouth

but now, nations of the world, I warn you
when you see my love
when you turn toward Jerusalem

you will say I bore all for him
the pain and loss was for him
I was his to the core

"But what makes your love any better than ours
what makes you so beautiful
that he leaves you, and you search for him?

How is your love better than any other
that you stoop from your ivory tower
daring to warn us?"

My love is white with radiance
red with vigorous strength
unmistakable—a banner leading the way

over the heads of a great army
and his head more inspiring than a crown of gold
his hair a raven-black flame

a dove's eyes, clear
beside a soothing river
reflecting its depth, brimming

pools of tenderness—
indestructible jewels
set in whites of kindness

his gaze a penetrating shaft of light
so deft
it is milk—warm and familiar

his words are riverbanks, firm
lush spice beds
a lingering perfume

to remind you of his lips
which are roses
his beard a soft bed of grass

to lean against like a page of his words
bathed in transparent dew
flowing with myrrh

his arms form a vessel of gold
to hold me secure
as a voyager to Tarshish

his will is a sail
and his desires
are a steady wind

his belly is polished ivory—
and strong, clear as azure
is his skin—a cloudless sky

his legs are firm columns
fine as marble
and his feet like golden pedestals—

columns of a scroll, words of spun gold—
his appearance naturally noble as
Lebanon cedars swaying in the breeze

his breath a delicious breeze
words a golden nectar
sustenance and delight

he is altogether delightful—
this is my love
and this my true friend

who never abandons me
a love so pure
you will know it unmistakably

when you turn toward Jerusalem
nations of the world
and all your sons and daughters.

ABOUT THE AUTHOR

David Rosenberg is a poet, essayist, and biblical scholar. He is the best known and most widely sought translator of the Hebrew Bible in our time. Mr. Rosenberg's work has appeared in *The Paris Review, Hudson Review, American Poetry Review, The New Republic, Harper's,* and *The Nation,* among other journals.

Born in Detroit in 1943, Mr. Rosenberg has taught literature and creative writing in Toronto and New York. After several years as an editor in Israel, he became senior editor at Harcourt Brace and editor in chief of the Jewish Publication Society, where he began his best-selling translation of the Bible's first great writer, *The Book of J.*

A Poet's Bible: Rediscovering the Voices of the Original Text won the PEN/Book-of-the-Month Club Translation Prize for 1992, the first English translation of the Bible to win a major literary award.

Mr. Rosenberg is currently editing *Writers in the Planetary Garden* and giving a course of the same title at the New School for Social Research, for teachers in the life and earth sciences in the New York area. The pilot project was designed for botanists at Fairchild Tropical Garden in Miami.

Advance praise for *The Lost Book of Paradise:*

"Breathtaking. . .a direct descendant of *Paradise Lost* in its wonder, its resonance, its concentration on human life in such a way as to convey eternal worlds beyond human knowledge. . .this is a major work."
—Grace Schulman, poetry editor of *The Nation*

"*The Lost Book of Paradise* is filled with the exquisite irony of one who knows how to imperil our simplest notion of belief. Rosenberg refuses to make it any easier for us than the suspenseful fictions of Borges, Kafka, or the J author herself." —David Shapiro, author of *To an Idea*

"David Rosenberg's *The Lost Book of Paradise* is an original, imaginative, and audacious work of art. Rosenberg is a gifted American poet who also writes concise and lucid vernacular prose. He has composed for our delight a fictive ancient Hebrew document and mythic poem in which our Mother, Eve, and the feminine aspect of the divine have been fused. *The Lost Book of Paradise* is a brilliant achievement." —Hugh Nissenson, author of *The Tree of Life*

Praise for David Rosenberg's previous books:

The Book of J

"A bold and deeply meditated translation." —Frank Kermode, *The New York Times Book Review*

"The play of J's language emerges in Rosenberg's version as it does not in King James.... What we are likeliest to miss in J when we read her previous translators is given back to us by Rosenberg."
—Harold Bloom

A Poet's Bible

"Rosenberg's music, simultaneously as new as the present moment and as old as the Bible's first authors, obliges those of us who read in English to look past our own beloved versions of the book and into the hearts of inspired ancient writing." —Judges' citation for the PEN/Book-of-the-Month Club Translation Prize for 1992

"Rosenberg's translations from the Hebrew scriptures are the best in this century without a doubt." —Hayden Carruth, *The Nation*

Printed in USA © 1993 Hyperion